THE TEN CO

By the same author:

The Trumpet in the Morning

Stuart Blanch
Archbishop of York

The Ten Commandments

Hodder and Stoughton
London   Sydney   Auckland   Toronto

British Library Cataloguing in Publication Data

Blanch, Stuart Y
　　The Ten Commandments
　　I. Commandments, Ten – Commentaries
　　I. Title
　　222'.16'06　　　BSI285.3

ISBN 0-340-27149-3

Hodder and Stoughton Editorial Office:
47 Bedford Square, London WC1B 3DP.

To my friends of the Jewish faith with whom I share a precious heritage for the healing of the nations.

CONTENTS

Author's Acknowledgements

In addition to the standard books, I have cause to be grateful to Dr. Anthony Phillips for his book *Israel's Criminal Law*, to Bishop John Spong for *The Living Commandments*, to Sir Norman Anderson for *God's Law and God's Love* and to Dr. Brevard Childs for his commentary on Exodus. I would also like to thank Dr. Caroline Rakestraw for producing and Mr. Michael Dawson for recording the original broadcasts and Mr. David Blunt, Miss Daphne Wood, Mrs. Val Smith and Mrs. Joyce Hall for helping to produce the finished script. My final word of thanks must be to Mr. Rob Warner, Senior Editor of Religious Books for Hodder and Stoughton, for his encouragement and for his careful oversight of the whole process. Other debts I no doubt owe but have long since forgotten to whom I owe them.

INTRODUCTION

The reader is entitled to an explanation about the
origins of this book. It began as a series of broadcasts for
the American radio network, under the sponsorship of
'The Episcopal Radio-TV Foundation' of Atlanta,
Georgia. They were produced and recorded by Dr.
Caroline Rakestraw, Executive Director of the
Foundation, in the language laboratories of York
University. I have removed the most blatant
colloquialisms but I have kept to the colloquial style and
have not removed all references to the American
audience for which they were originally intended. As
anyone with any experience of these matters will know, it
is as difficult to transform a colloquial style into a literary
style as to make a literary style suitable for speaking or
broadcasting. So, broadcast addresses they remain,
partial, selective, personal.

But the real origins of the book lie further back. Several
years ago Mr. England, then of Hodder and Stoughton,
asked me to produce a book on the Ten Commandments
and I did what could have been the ground work for it in
my own book *The Trumpet in the Morning* which was 'a
study of law and freedom today in the light of the
Hebraeo-Christian tradition'. For the benefit of the
reader who is not familiar with that book, I have
summarised the arguments in Chapter 1 of the book you
now have in your hands.

But I doubt whether I would ever have attempted a
book on the Ten Commandments, as such, had it not
been for the invitation from the Episcopal Radio-TV

Foundation – partly because I did not find the subject attractive, partly because I felt I did not have the necessary technical equipment or training at my disposal. Surely this was a task for the moral theologian, the jurist or the moral philosopher.

When, therefore, I agreed to do the series of broadcasts I did so on the basis of a rather different view of my task from the one I had originally entertained. I did not see myself as a moral theologian or a jurist building an elaborate code of ethics upon the Ten Commandments but as an expositor of the principles underlying the Ten Commandments in the minds of the Hebrew people, in the hope of making those Commandments relevant to the moral and social needs of our own time. This was a less ambitious project but troublesome just the same, because it is by no means easy to arrive at a confident opinion about what the Ten Commandments meant to the Hebrew people at various stages of their history; without that confidence it is not easy to apply them with confidence to the issues of the present day. Moreover, the addresses could hardly be loaded with heavy academic material for a radio network in which instant understanding is the order of the day.

I therefore chose a method of handling the subject which was suggested by the title given to the original addresses – 'The End of a Golden String'. The quotation is from William Blake and the whole verse runs:

I give you the end of a golden string,
Only wind it into a ball
It will lead you in at Heaven's gate
Built in Jerusalem's wall

The addresses, therefore, made no claim to be an exhaustive discussion of the Ten Commandments based on an imposing array of learning and precedent. They were intended rather to put in the hands of individual readers 'the end of a golden string' – the merest suggestion of how individuals and societies might take their cue from the revelation to Moses about the way we ought to conduct our own lives and about the objectives we ought to seek for society.

It would be hardly possible to treat the subject in this way without appealing to one who was Himself a Jew and is, for Christians, the final arbiter in all matters of human life and conduct, viz. Jesus of Nazareth. Jesus was a radical teacher of the law and at the same time a doughty protagonist for freedom, a man who was more concerned with attitudes than with acts, a man who saw human relationships as a refraction of our ultimate relationship with God Himself.

The figure of the young man who came to Jesus asking how he might find eternal life haunts the pages of this book as he haunts my own mind. Here indeed was a seeker after truth, looking for eternal life, who had not been able to find it within the moral and intellectual structures of his own faith. Jesus as a teacher of the law could be expected to quote from the Ten Commandments, and He did so. But He did more. He summoned the young man to a personal discipleship which far transcended the cultivation of ethical values or sedulous application to the letter of the law.

The illustration on the cover is Rembrandt's picture of Moses depicted as he is about to break the tablets of the law. In another sense we have been breaking the law ever since and, so I believe, we see the consequences in our own lives and in the life of society around us. These chapters are no more than an attempt to suggest ways in

11

which we may recover our reverence for this ancient law and learn to live by it in the glorious freedom which Christ has conferred upon us.

1 LAW AND FREEDOM

There is an old story that some time after the devil rebelled against God and was cast out of heaven, he was asked what he missed most from his life in heaven. The devil thought for a few moments and then replied – 'I miss most the sound of the trumpet in the morning.' What the devil did he mean, I ask myself. He had chosen to reign in hell rather than serve in heaven. He had preferred to be a law unto himself instead of an observer of the law of God. He had decided to pursue his own objectives rather than the objectives which God had prescribed for him. In short, he was 'free'. But what did he miss, what was this sound of the trumpet?

I joined the Royal Air Force as a young man of twenty-two, after four years of more or less doing what I wanted to do – working in an insurance office but choosing my own pleasures and my own friends and largely in charge of my own time. Joining the Services was a bit of a shock and with many of my fellow recruits I did not take easily to the raucous cry of the sergeant in the morning, nor to the endless drill, nor to the church parades, nor to the kit inspections, nor to the thousand and one absurd regulations (as they seemed to us) which governed our lives and restricted our liberty. So it was just bliss to get a week's leave, to get up in the morning when I felt like it, to wear what I liked, to go where I wished, in short, to be free. But, I have to admit, when the leave was over, it was with almost a sense of relief that I

13

climbed back into uniform and resumed the ordered life of an RAF station. Clearly, I missed the sound of the trumpet. I found it burdensome to be free.

I spent six years in the Air Force, undistinguished years in terms of contribution to the war effort, but highly fruitful in other ways. For one thing I became a practising Christian during that time and for another I enjoyed a kind of inner freedom which I have never enjoyed since. Within the limitations of a highly structured organisation, I moved freely. I walked at liberty. I had learnt the truth, expressed by Wordsworth in his 'Ode to Duty' –

Me this unchartered freedom tires,
I feel the weight of chance desires.

What is true of the individual could be true of society as a whole. We in the West have all felt the effects of the so-called permissive society in which freedom is defined as the freedom to run your own life in your own way, regardless of moral law or social convention or the welfare of others. At the same time, and perhaps not surprisingly, we have seen the rise of highly authoritarian regimes in which the freedom of the individual counts for little or nothing. A recent report tells us that there are 127 nation states in the world and 97 of them are dictatorships or single-party systems. By tomorrow there could be 98 or 99 or 100 so swiftly are our freedoms being extinguished on the face of the earth.

It must be obvious that there is a tension between the perfectly legitimate freedoms of the subject and the responsibility of any government for an ordered society. The Duke of Edinburgh once said that if things are to go on as they are at the moment, we shall soon need a licence to breathe.

In a complex society regulations multiply. We in England must drive on the left, a very sensible precaution and one that is absolutely necessary if we are to keep alive. I cannot build a house without planning permission. In some parts of Old England I cannot even change the shape of a window without planning permission; I cannot chop down a tree, I cannot put up a shed.

The unintended result of all this is to build up a certain resistance to any notion of authority. The man who is caught by a police speed trap resents the policeman. The tradesman who has infringed some obscure regulation in the conduct of his business resents the magistrate who imposes the fine. The honest householder who makes a mistake in his income tax return is embittered by what he suffers from that unhappy representative of central government, the tax collector. And so in all sorts of trivial ways, a resistance to all notions of authority is built up.

At the same time, positive and deliberate acts of lawlessness increase – in the streets, on the campus, at the factory gate; men are afraid to walk the streets at night, women double lock their doors and big businessmen employ bodyguards against the risk of kidnapping. In our hearts, we all long for what we imagine to be a stable society, intelligently structured and sensitively controlled, in which we may walk abroad about our daily business with a certain sense of freedom. We may not enjoy the sound of the trumpet ourselves, but we recognise its necessity if we are to live together in anything approaching a civilised society.

My experience in the Air Force, often repeated in my subsequent life, and my experience of society, such as it

15

is, has caused me to consider the status of law in the ordering of human life. Dr. Friedman said in the *New York Times* a few years ago;

> The rule of law does not guarantee freedom, since general laws can be tyrannical. But increasing reliance on the rule of law clearly played a major role in transforming Western society from a world in which the ordinary citizen was literally subject to the arbitrary will of his master, to a world in which the ordinary citizen could regard himself as his own master.

'Amen' to that, Dr. Friedman.

By a curious paradox, it is only the rule of law, widely accepted and generally recognised, which can preserve our freedoms. That is why in this series of sermons I am turning to the Ten Commandments for guidance. You may well say that they come from a past age (true), that they are irrelevant or (the most disparaging response) that they are simplistic. What, after all, can a set of rules, dating from the beginnings of an unimportant nomadic tribe called the Hebrews, say to us, members of a highly sophisticated civilisation, burdened with problems which the Hebrews never even dreamt of?

But, in a way, these also constitute the reasons for their importance. They do indeed come from a past age, but they have played an enormously important role in the creation of the legal systems of the West. They seem, it is true, irrelevant to the more sophisticated forms of decision-making which we have to employ, but they deal with aspects of human nature which are as relevant to us now as they were to our Hebrew forefathers.

They are, of course, simplistic, in so far as they consist

of a series of do's or dont's; they recognise only two colours — black and white. They propose only two alternatives — good or bad. But perhaps in a so-called permissive society, that is what we need to hear and perhaps in a society where our freedoms are always in danger of being extinguished, that is what governments need to hear as well. So I make no apologies for turning back to this ancient source of wisdom and morality.

The giving of the Ten Commandments was a stupendous experience in the mind of the Hebrew writers.

> When the people saw the thunder and lightning and heard the trumpet and saw the mountain in smoke, they trembled with fear. They stayed at a distance and said to Moses, "Speak to us yourself and we will listen. But do not have God speak to us or we will die."
>
> Moses said to the people, "Do not be afraid. God has come to test you, so that the fear of God will be with you to keep you from sinning." The people remained at a distance, while Moses approached the thick darkness where God was.
>
> (Exodus 20: 18–21)

We have no means of rationalising or even explaining the extraordinary events surrounding the giving of the Ten Commandments. They lie, buried in the history of the race, beyond recall. But what we can be sure about is that those events made an ineffaceable impression upon the life and the literature of Israel. The giving of the law to Moses was the most important event in their history and (they dared to believe) the most important event in the history of the world. For it was there that God spoke like the sound of the trumpet, not only to the Hebrew people

17

but to all mankind, offering us all a law by which to abide and a way in which to walk.

But perhaps the word 'law' is misleading, giving an impression of God as an implacable legislator, handing down laws which had to be minutely observed on pain of death, seeking to restrict and inhibit us from all things we really enjoy.

The original Hebrew word does not suggest that at all. It is a word meaning to teach, suggesting not a judge seated on his throne in heaven but a father teaching his son to walk, telling him how to avoid dangers, helping him to understand himself in his relationship with others. 'When Israel was a child I loved him,' the prophet Hosea said, 'and out of Egypt I called my son.'

We in the modern world need guidelines for life, just as surely as the Hebrews needed guidelines for their life in the wilderness. Our wilderness is more complicated but it is just as dangerous. I find it a solemn and alarming thought that I have only one life to live and one serious mistake can ruin it. God in His mercy has provided us with certain guidelines or signposts which, if they do no more, offer us boundaries within which we may freely move without fear or restraint. To operate within the limitations set by God in the Ten Commandments is the secret of the only freedom we shall ever enjoy on earth. His service, so the old collect goes, is perfect freedom.

The Hebrews exchanged their bondage in Egypt for bondage to the living God. Because of that, Tevye, the patriarchal figure of the musical *Fiddler on the Roof* says, 'Everyone knows who he is and what he has to do.'

Broadly speaking, there are two ways of dealing with the Ten Commandments. The first is one which has produced the highly developed Judaism of our own day. These commandments came to be regarded as the basis of the whole ethical and religious system of Israel by which every act was monitored, every contingency provided for – what you should eat and what you should wear, and why, what you were to say when you went to bed and what you were to say when you got up, how you were to conduct your business, how you were to treat your servants.

Over the generations between the giving of the law at Sinai and the coming of Jesus, one thousand five hundred years later, the Ten Commandments had been elaborated by generations of scribes into a huge body of literature, so profuse and so complicated that only the learned or leisured could begin to cope with it. By the time of our Lord, the law had developed into a complicated system, far removed from the ten simple commandments. It had become a burden rather than a blessing and God had become a judge rather than a father. No detail of life was out of range of His all-seeing eye. No act went unrecorded. Those original signposts in the desert had been buried under mountains of debate and controversy, rule and precedent, regulations and laws.

That is why our Lord's teaching has a certain ambivalence about it. He honoured the law and warned His hearers that not one jot or tittle of the law would pass away. He revered the figure of Moses and often appealed to the original tradition of Moses over against the later refinements of those who sat in Moses's seat. But He was at pains to set the people free. And when Jesus climbed the mountain of the Beatitudes, like Moses of old, to receive the word of God and to communicate it to the masses, He did not preach like the scribes, quoting the Scriptures, appealing to precedent, giving examples, counselling adherence to the law. He went back behind the law of His day to the law of God, which He summarised in two immortal sentences, both of them to be found in the Old Testament but not originally associated with each other.

> Love the Lord your God with all your heart and with all your soul and with all your mind and with all your strength ... Love your neighbour as yourself.
>
> (Mark 12:30–31)

All His parables were in one way or another illustrations of this theme. The Parable of the Prodigal Son, the most famous of all, unveiled the real relationship between God and His people. Who could doubt the prodigal's love for his father after that astonishing welcome home? The Parable of the Good Samaritan illustrated how the call for humanity transcends all boundaries of religion and race.

Jesus criticised the Church leaders of His day because they bound heavy burdens upon the poor. That is to say they sought to impose regulations which were quite impossible to fulfil for those engaged in the everyday business of trade and commerce and industry. He offered instead a royal road of freedom. He enunciated certain cardinal examples of conduct but within those limits called people to attend to the word of God themselves, to listen for the voice that said to them 'This is the way, walk in it.' He reminded them of the Good Shepherd in heaven who, if they were willing, would lead His flock tenderly and surely into green pastures. He spoke to them of a father who had the best interests of his children at heart and for their own good made His will known to them. He gave them 'the end of a golden string'.

This is a quotation from the works of the great English

poet, artist and man of letters, William Blake. Blake would turn in his grave, or even revolve in his grave, if he thought that words of his were being used in a series of sermons on the Ten Commandments because he wholly abhorred systems and dogmatic structures, ethical codes and rules of conduct. But perhaps I could reassure him in heaven, if he is tuned in to the right station, that I do not intend to use the Ten Commandments in this way at all. The Ten Commandments are best seen, not as the foundation of a vast superstructure of ideas, but as a simple basis for everyday life.

To us some of the Commandments appear to relate to our duty to God and some of them to our duty to our neighbour. Moses would not have seen them like that. For him the responsibility to neighbours was part of the total responsibility to God Himself. The Commandments are about God and how we may know Him, love Him, serve Him and, by His grace, find the way through *our* wilderness to *our* promised land, to *our* Jerusalem.

All I shall be attempting to do is to put into your hands the end of a golden string and it is for you to wind it into a ball. We all have our moments, of crisis, of hesitation, of panic. As a navigator in the Air Force I know what it feels like to be lost. These experiences can be destructive or constructive. They can unhinge your mind and undermine your health. They can destroy your relationships with others, they can make you a burden to your friends. But they can also be the means of discovery, a way of life. They can be the end of a golden string. At all costs keep hold of it and wind it into a ball.

2 THE FIRST COMMANDMENT

I am the Lord your God, who brought you out of
Egypt, out of the land of slavery. You shall have
no other gods before me.

(Exodus 20:2, 3)

The Hebrews were not philosophers. The Hebrew
god was not the god of the philosophers. He was the god
which brought them out of the land of Egypt, out of the
land of slavery. He was a god of everyday life, a god of
the battle and a god of the crisis. He was a god not merely
to be thought about or talked about but to be obeyed.
'You shall have no other gods before me.' There is a lot of
difference between 'talking about' and 'believing in' as I
discovered when I was invited to an RAF station in
Yorkshire shortly after I became Archbishop of York.

The particular RAF station I visited was one upon
which was based the Air Sea Rescue Unit whose tasks
varied from picking up a sheep which had fallen over the
cliff to rescuing men from a stricken trawler breaking up
on the rocks. A few weeks before I visited the station one
of the helicopter crews in gale force winds had been called
out for just such a rescue. The trawler was breaking up on
the rocks at the foot of the cliff. The pilot had to hover his
helicopter below the level of the cliff to try and counteract
not only the gale blowing in from the sea, but also the
huge turbulence which built up at clifftop level. The

winchman had to be let down on his wire and then swung gently to and fro until he could reach the trawler. They performed this operation not once but nineteen times and every man was rescued. It was an exercise of matchless skill and dauntless courage and the pilot was justly awarded the George Cross for gallantry.

I commented on this great feat at lunch-time and the commanding officer replied that as a matter of fact there was going to be an air sea rescue practice that very afternoon. Would I like to go on it? 'I would be delighted,' I said. He went on to say, 'We wondered whether you might like to be rescued?' I felt distinctly less delighted and I asked what he meant. 'Well,' he said, 'we will take you out into the North Sea and lower you down on to a launch (a dry run he called it), then we will pick you up again.'

Now, I was not a stranger to aeroplanes because I had been a navigator during the war but this was something new to me. So not without trepidation I waved goodbye to my wife on the tarmac and set off eastwards to the North Sea. Of course there was nothing to worry about. I was with the most competent crew on the unit, the pilot had had thousands of hours of experience and he had just won a George Cross. The navigator looked the gnarled old type who had had plenty of experience and the winchman was young and athletic enough to give anyone confidence. In theory I had nothing to fear.

In practice I was not a little nervous, especially when I sat on the ledge of the helicopter with my feet dangling in space waiting to be swung out on the end of a wire. The navigator had huge gloves on his hands. 'Why?' I asked him amidst the din of the helicopter engine. His reply was the kind I might well have expected from a member of the Air Force. 'That,' he said, 'is to catch hold of the wire if it breaks.'

So I reached the launch, spent a quarter of an hour or so on it and then the winchman swooped down again and took me off. Almost by instinct I clung to him as a drowning man clings to his rescuer. But he just laughed and flapped his arms in the air to signify that I was quite secure on the end of the line. And then real enjoyment took over from anxiety. I too flapped my arms in the air, let go and was content to hang between heaven and earth until I reached the helicopter and was pushed back into it.

For me this story exactly illustrates the difference between what you might call a theoretical belief and a practical belief. It was one thing to know that the crew was competent and the helicopter reliable. It was quite another thing to submit yourself wholly to their care, to depend on them for your life. The fact that I am alive now is proof that my practical faith was vindicated.

Something like this distinguishes the genuinely religious man from the theorist. It was something like this which distinguished the Hebrews from most of their contemporaries. The god they worshipped was the god who had brought them out of the land of slavery, had enabled them to cross the Red Sea in the face of appalling danger, had guarded them in the wilderness against the twin enemies of famine and thirst, had kept their enemies at bay and had spoken to them in the thunders and lightnings of Sinai.

That is why the first commandment *is* the first commandment. The commandments are not a series of regulations designed to make us good or to make us happy, or even to control our vices. They are intimately associated with an experience of the ineffable God, the Creator of the universe, the Lord and Master of all life. They are at least as much about our relationship with

25

God as they are about our relationship with other people.

You cannot pick and choose. You cannot disbelieve in God and at the same time honour what you take to be His Commandments. Once remove the Commandments from their primal source and they become something else. They may be useful, they may indeed be essential, but they are not commandments which emerged from the thunders and lightnings of Sinai.

If we are to understand this first and great Commandment we need, however, to come to terms with certain difficulties in it. The first one is the opening phrase itself 'I am the Lord your God.' The words for God are not synonymous and they represent two different Hebrew words. This distinction has to be understood if the Commandment is to be understood. The word 'Elohim', if I may put it simply, stands for the Universal Creator instinctively known to all and honoured not only by the nation of Israel but by other nations as well. The word 'Jahwe' is the name for God given to Moses at the Burning Bush. 'Tell the Israelites,' God said to Moses, 'that it is Jahwe, the God of their forefathers, the God of Abraham and the God of Isaac, the God of Jacob, who has sent you to them.'

So when you next hear the Commandments read in Church just observe whether the reader has it right. He should be saying to you with as much emphasis as he can contrive, 'I am the Lord *your* God.' There are, as St. Paul said, 'many gods and many lords' (1 Corinthians 8:5). Thus the Israelites are to understand that the God who is now speaking to them is their God (Jahwe), the God who has brought them out of Egypt, out of the land of slavery.

The second difficulty relates to the following phrase 'you shall have no other gods before me.' This is the translation from the New International Version; other modern Bibles offer us a variety of choice. For example the New English Bible reads. 'You shall have no other god to set against me.' The Good News Bible offers 'Worship no god but me' and this is roughly the same in the Jerusalem Bible.

But the Hebrew word translated 'before me' means strictly and almost invariably in ordinary speech 'in my presence'. It was a phrase used for being in the presence of a king or the presence of your employer, or the presence of your wife and children, or the presence of your creditor, or (to strike a more cheerful note) in the presence of your benefactor. Taken therefore in its literal sense, this verse seems likely to mean that no shrine at which Jahwe, the God of Israel, is worshipped, must be used for the worship of any other 'god'.

Now this will seem odd to us but it was a real and desperate issue in the ancient world. When the Roman Emperor wished to set up his standards in the holy place of the Temple of Jerusalem, he aroused fanatical resistance from the Jews. He was not insisting that they worshipped him alone. In the easy-going religious manners of the day, you could worship a whole series of gods without offending any of them. But for the Hebrews this would have been to infringe the first and greatest command of all – no other gods were to be worshipped in association with Jahwe.

One can understand the bewilderment of the Roman legionaries who encountered such fanatical resistance from the Jews. For them, the worship of many gods would have been regarded as a kind of insurance policy. There were no policies against theft or loss of crops or hazards of travel or earthquakes or flood in those days, but men still needed the securities that such policies are supposed to provide. So they were prepared to worship any god who might appear to be useful to them in their daily life — the sun upon which they were wholly dependent, the moon and the stars which were thought to control the affairs of the earth, the god of the rivers, the god of the hills, the god of the forests, the god of war, the god of sex without which no procreation could be achieved.

There were indeed, in St. Paul's time, lords many and gods many, and his sermon at Athens reflected the situation as he stood in the midst of Mars hill and said:

> Men of Athens: I see that in every way you are religious. For as I walked round and observed your objects of worship, I even found an altar with this inscription:
> TO AN UNKNOWN GOD.
>
> (Acts 17:22–23)

Athenians were, in common with all the cities of the ancient world, hedging their bets — they did not wish to miss anyone out who might be of use to them.

This was the world in which the Jewish people struggled, and struggled fanatically, to preserve the purity of their religion and to keep the first Commandment. For that reason they were regarded as very odd people but they were only being loyal to the first and greatest of the Commandments which they had received at Sinai.

But you may be asking the question — 'what on earth has this to do with us?' We no longer live in that ancient world, the polytheists of our day are confined to a few primitive tribes in the jungle of Central America. We do not bow down before sticks and stones and trees. We do

28

not light candles or burn incense before the god of travel or the god of sex or the god of fertility or the god of war.

Perhaps we ought not to be too sure. The famous theologian Paul Tillich said, 'Your god is that reality which elicits from you your deepest feelings and your most ultimate concern.' To what, may I ask you, do your deepest feelings attach? And what is your most ultimate concern? If you are a member of the Church you may stand with the congregation and say with sincerity – 'I believe in one God.' But do you perhaps permit other 'gods' in your pantheon? In the shrine of your heart, do you perhaps harbour other 'deities' which, if you are honest, inspire your deepest feeling and constitute your ultimate concern? If so, you are a polytheist and this first command stands over against you as a giant challenge to your way of life.

Of course you do not bow down to the sticks and stones, of course you do not have in your house an altar to an unknown god, but, as I know to my cost, there are still lords many and gods many at work in our lives, sometimes indeed responsible for the occasional confusions which so distress us. You may indeed profess faith in one god but your 'ultimate concern' may be work, or power, or success, or popularity, or your own pet doctrine, or your reputation as a radical. You are, in all but name, a polytheist.

This does not just apply to us as individuals any more than the original Commandment did. The Ten Commandments were part of a covenant with the whole people of Israel, with far-reaching implications for the way in which they ordered society. Disobedience to God's command by society brought with it as serious consequences to society as disobedience by an individual brought to an individual. The prophets of Israel never

29

tired of saying this and the people of Israel never tired of disregarding them. The collapse of Samaria and the destruction of Jerusalem were seen as consequences of this disobedience. Any nation which worships 'other gods', however sophisticated it may be and however unaware of the issues involved, comes under the same judgement.

There is a passage in St. Mark's Gospel which expresses this Old Testament truth in New Testament terms. It says:

> As Jesus started on his way, a man ran up to him and fell on his knees before him. "Good teacher," he asked, "what must I do to inherit eternal life?"
>
> "Why do you call me good?" Jesus answered. "No-one is good – except God alone. You know the commandments: Do not murder, do not commit adultery, do not steal, do not give false testimony, do not defraud, honour your father and mother."
>
> "Teacher," he declared, "all these I have kept since I was a boy."
>
> Jesus looked at him and loved him. "One thing you lack," he said. "Go, sell everything you have and give to the poor, and you will have treasure in heaven. Then come, follow me."
>
> At this the man's face fell. He went away sad, because he had great wealth.
>
> (Mark 10: 17–22)

The 'punch-line' if I may put it thus is in the words 'follow me'. It was not sufficient for this stranger to go on being a good boy. He exactly exemplifies Paul Tillich's words – 'Your god is that reality which elicits from you your

30

deepest feeling and your most ultimate concern.' He was a man of great possessions. He was a polytheist. He believed that he was worshipping the god of Abraham, Isaac and Jacob but, in the shrine of his own heart, there were other gods as well – his great possessions.

So when he encounters God's representative on earth in the person of Jesus Christ his true spiritual state is exposed. He was not prepared to give up his other gods, his securities on earth to follow the God and Father of our Lord Jesus Christ, which would infallibly have led him to heaven's gate (eternal life as he put it). He left the end of the golden string lying on the ground and went sorrowfully away. I fear that his sorrows continued with him to the end of his days.

We have to choose between the God who brought Israel out of Egypt, out of the land of slavery, the God and Father of our Lord Jesus Christ, and the many gods who clamour for our attention. We may be long past the stage when we worshipped pop idols or football players. We may even have passed the stage when we bow down before the gods of wealth and status, but no man in this life is ever quite immune to temptation. He can never afford to ignore the first and great Commandment.

I have worshipped all sorts of gods in my time. As a child, I am told, I worshipped my father. As a schoolboy I worshipped the young 'goddess' whom I used to pass every morning as I cycled to school. As a young man I know I worshipped Wally Hammond, the captain of the English cricket team, and I would go miles just to watch him walk out from the pavilion to the wicket; it would break my heart if all too soon he was walking from the wicket back to the pavilion. There is a sense in which I worshipped my great woolly Scottish collie dog. And unhappily, my impression is that as we get older our gods tend to get smaller — our meaningless habits born of a lifetime, our foibles of food or dress, our superstitions, our prejudices.

You may pride yourself like the young man of the gospels that you have not committed murder or adultery, you do not steal and you have not given false evidence, you do not defraud and you honour your father and your mother. But he will be a bold man or a singularly insensitive one who can be confident that he has not disobeyed the first Commandment.

This has a perfectly practical bearing upon our everyday life. To worship many gods is to live a divided life, drawn this way and that by conflicting desires and conflicting ambitions. We try to do opposite things with our lives and suffer the penalty in our minds and our bodies. To worship the one true God is to be on the way to a certain harmony. Our interests gather round this ultimate concern. We are at peace with ourselves and are therefore more likely to be at peace with others. I become one person when I worship one God.

In your particular wilderness you may hear His word, follow His directions and look forward with joy to *your* promised land. You have the end of a golden string which will ultimately lead you into heaven's gate built in Jerusalem's wall. Hang on to that golden string for God's sake and for your own.

3 THE SECOND COMMANDMENT

You shall not make for yourself a graven image.
(Exodus 20: 4)

You may know the story of the American sailor who, having heard the Ten Commandments recited in Church, said to his friend as they went out, 'Well at least I have never made a graven image.' It was probably true, but if he had known the New Testament particularly well, not all that comforting. For St. James says 'Whoever keeps the whole law and yet stumbles at just one point is guilty of breaking all of it.' (James 2:10) He was taking refuge, as we all do, in the knowledge of the sins he had not committed, to excuse those he had.

I can think of many occasions when visiting a patient in hospital and the patient has said to me, 'I can't think why I should suffer like this because I have never done anyone any harm.' I recognise the feeling and of course would never think of disputing it with a patient in hospital but it is a bold assertion to make, considering the tangle of relationships in which we are all involved and of our inevitable unawareness of the effect we have on other people. But for the moment let us concentrate on the graven image.

As in the other Commandments, it is essential to know what is actually being said, and we must look at this term 'graven image' and ask in what sense it was used by the original writer. It translates a Hebrew word 'pesel' which is used fifty-two times in the Old Testament and very frequently in the Prophets. It meant originally anything carved from wood or stone, but later came to include metal figures as well. There is another word normally translated 'idol' and it is the Hebrew word 'g'lul' which likewise occurs about fifty times in the Old Testament. They can be used interchangeably but there is a distinction because 'g'lul' originally meant log, i.e. something uncarved, shapeless, like the trunk of an ancient tree or a hunk of stone from a mountainside, or less common a meteorite.

When you add in all the other Hebrew words which are variously translated image or idol in our English translations, you would have between one-and two-hundred indirect references to this Commandment. Some of the finest passages in the prophetic literature and some of the most vitriolic are addressed to this subject. Take this, for example, from the book of Isaiah,

> To whom, then, will you compare God?
> What image will you compare him to?
> As for an idol, a craftsman casts it,
> and a goldsmith overlays it with gold
> and fashions silver chains for it.
> A man too poor to present such an offering
> selects wood that will not rot.
> He looks for a skilled craftsman to set up
> an idol that will not topple.

(Isaiah 40 : 18–20)

So the American sailor may not himself ever have made a graven image but it was obviously a constant temptation to the people of Israel. Law and prophet, psalms and

34

proverbs, early literature and late literature abound with references to and prohibitions of this practice. We are bound to ask the question 'Why?', and I am offering a few suggestions, based largely on the Scriptures themselves, from which we may rather surprisingly infer that the temptations to idolatory are not confined to the ancient world. Perhaps the American sailor had made a few images for himself, even if they were not graven or carved.

It is important to associate the second Commandment with the first because if you are to insist on the worship of one God then the graven image is likely to prove a constant temptation. It would not be long before the image of Jahwe would be followed by other images in His shrine. The old insurance instinct would soon have prevailed – if Jahwe had failed to protect them they must look for someone else. If the crops had failed it might be necessary to find Jahwe a consort who could occupy the shrine with Him, before whom votive offerings could be made in pursuit of a better harvest or successful conception.

It would not be long before the shrine of Jahwe would look like a model of an Eastern Court – the king indeed distinguished by superior workmanship and better attire and more majestic size, but surrounded by a whole range of lesser deities. The polytheism which had gone out at the front door would have come in at the back.

For the same reason the Commandment does not only forbid the carved image of Jahwe Himself but 'the likeness of anything in heaven above or on the earth beneath or in the waters below'. So deep rooted in the minds of the Hebrew people was this prohibition that for a people who have contributed so richly to the culture of the world they have contributed comparatively little to the plastic arts. Musicians, mathematicians, poets, novelists, scientists, abound but of Jewish sculptors and portrait painters there are few. It was this prohibition which perhaps above everything else made Israel, in the ancient world, a peculiar people.

The legionaries who broke into the Holy of Holies when Jerusalem was destroyed must have been astonished to find nothing there − no image, carved or uncarved, no representations. They were used to shrines richly provided with examples of the plastic arts, offering gods to meet every need, providing a wide range of options for the worshipper.

We may thus, in one way, account for the Commandment but how do we account for the extraordinary fidelity to it and the important place it has occupied in the life of Israel? Is there an historical moment which, as it were, justifies it? If there is any such historical moment it can only be the one associated with Sinai itself, where it is perfectly clear that God's voice was heard but His form was not seen. He spoke to Moses 'in a thick cloud'. 'Go down,' He said, 'and warn the people they do not force their way through to see the Lord.' (Exodus 19:20)

The Moses who came down from the mountain did not come down with a visible representation of God but with ten words on two tablets of stone. God had chosen to reveal Himself by His *Word*. The task of communicating the reality of God to the people was entrusted to prophets not to artificers or connoisseurs of the fine arts. The third reason for the prohibition is this. An image fixes the object it is supposed to represent in a form inevitably peculiar to a particular culture, a particular country or a particular era. God does not change but He reveals Himself, or seeks so to do, in the appropriate categories of the day. An image constructed in the wilderness of Sinai would not have been very much use in the ghettoes of a sophisticated city like Alexandria. An idol fashioned in ancient Babylon would be of little significance for the modern Jewish community of New York. The idol before which the countryman feels at home would scarcely be the idol of the townsman.

Jahwe is the God of all history, not just of Biblical history, the God of all people, not just of Jewish people. Immutable Himself, He cannot be represented on earth in a *form* which is immutable, because the world changes and fashions are transient.

The last two reasons may be of less significance but are of some importance in understanding the mentality of an ancient people. The graven image limits God's freedom. The name Jahwe can mean 'I am what I am' or 'I shall become what I shall become'. The sovereign of all the earth enjoys a royal freedom to be Himself.

I take an example from my own experience. Archbishops have a certain 'image'. I get letters from disappointed correspondents who say that they came to York Minster but did not see me; they apparently have the image of an Archbishop who spends his day attired in cope and mitre sitting on his episcopal throne.

For others, more worldly, the image is of a wealthy prelate luxuriating in his great palace at Bishopthorpe, surrounded by servants, seated in lofty isolation in his study overlooking the River Ouse.

For others, the image is of a managing director with a battery of telephones in front of him, entirely absorbed with ecclesiastical business.

The fact of the matter is that the bulk of my engagements are, if we have to use the term, 'secular'. I spend as much time giving lectures to secular bodies or writing articles for secular newspapers as I do attending to ecclesiastical affairs. The image could limit my freedom to be myself and, what is even worse, I could become like the image which other people have created for me.

The last reason is that the graven image renders God powerless. It was assumed in the ancient world, and indeed well on into the Roman Empire, that every nation had its own tutelar deity who had a special responsibility for guarding the people from military defeat and was represented very often on the field of battle by an image or a standard. The Hebrews themselves once took the Ark onto the field of battle in the hope of ensuring the presence of their deity. The only trouble was that they lost the Ark and lost the battle.

So to be represented by a graven image is to submit the sovereign Lord of all creation to the risk of defeat, or at least seeming defeat. He is at the mercy of men, He has to be carried about, propped up, repaired, renovated. He cannot hear, He cannot smell, He cannot speak. He is powerless.

The sailor said – 'I have not made a graven image.' True enough. But what image of God does he carry about with him – a grandfather figure in Heaven, a remorseless judge, a tyrant, an emperor with a diminishing retinue, or as Koestler calls Him 'a ghost in the machine'. What image of God do you carry about?

There has been a striking illustration of this recently in a film called *Oh God*. It is the story of how a supermarket manager had a revelation from God. He was summoned to meet Him on the twenty-fifth floor of a certain block of flats where he was confronted with God – a God who looked rather like the caretaker. On another occasion God appeared to the manager as a street-cleaner and on another as a taxi driver. I saw the film in Vancouver in company with many other clergy who were attending a conference. It was a very amusing film – and in its way a moving one too. But I learnt to my surprise that it had been received in certain parts of the Church here with howls of wrath and had virtually to be withdrawn.

Now I ask myself why was it so bitterly opposed? There was certainly nothing blasphemous about it and I found the figure of God, played by the famous old actor George Burns, infinitely appealing. Suppose, I ask myself, God had been represented as a handyman in the block of flats? Would that perhaps have been better? Or a carpenter? One is driven to the conclusion that the objectors to the film had an image of God which made the film repulsive to them. Perhaps their image of God was of a mighty prelate in cope and mitre sitting on a heavenly throne or of a judge handing down sentences, or of a general at the head of a mighty army.

The fact of the matter was that when the Word did become flesh He became a handyman, a carpenter, and could just as well have become a taxi driver or a caretaker. That is why, perhaps, Paul dares to speak of Christ in Colossians 1, verse 15 as 'the image of the invisible God, the firstborn over all creation'. That was indeed a daring thing for a Jew to say, given the prohibition of images which had so long dominated the life of his people. But he was being true to our Lord's own words – 'he that has seen me has seen the Father.'

The only image which we are permitted which does not fall under the prohibition of the second Commandment is the image of a man, a Jewish man, with a face and an accent and a way of speaking, and a profession; a man royally free, who walked at liberty in the world – healing, commanding, liberating, reconciling. It is the image of the crucified *man* which dominates the Church, and although it may not always recognise it, dominates the world as well.

Some of you may be familiar with the famous readings from St. Mark performed by the renowned English actor Alec McCowen. In one of our English newspapers he described how the programme came into being. He was a very successful actor with a great reputation but he somehow came to feel trapped in his profession. He needed something else to do. Oddly enough, for one who is having to learn his lines all the time, he decided to learn the Gospel of St. Mark by heart. It took him a few months but in the end he got it word perfect.

And then it occurred to him that this might be capable of stage presentation. A courageous theatre management agreed and he appeared on the stage, dressed in slacks and sports coat. The only props were a table and a chair and a paperback version of St. Mark's Gospel, to which he never referred. It was an instant success and he has been doing it to crowded auditoriums on both sides of the Atlantic ever since.

He was kind enough to do it for the Lambeth Bishops assembled for the Lambeth Conference in 1978 in Canterbury, and I well remember his opening remarks to us:

> It is normal for there to be several actors on the stage with one prompter in the wings. Tonight I find myself in a different situation – one actor on the stage and five hundred prompters in the auditorium.

When writing about the effects of this enterprise on himself, this is what he had to say in the newspaper:

Whether or not you are "a believer" it is impossible to study St. Mark carefully and not *know* — without any shadow of doubt — that something amazing happened in Galilee two thousand years ago.

It was this strange prompting to learn St. Mark's Gospel by heart that was, for Alec McCowen, 'the end of a golden string'; it is obvious he is still winding it into a ball. God revealed himself to Alec McCowen not in an image but in a living man, the *Word* made flesh.

4 THE THIRD COMMANDMENT

You shall not misuse the name of the Lord your God.

(Exodus 20:7)

The Jewish commentary which I use gives as a subtitle to this third Commandment – 'against perjury and profane swearing'. Perjury is a serious offence in any civilised society as it perverts justice and threatens the liberty and even the life of another person. Profane swearing attracts its own penalties. You can be sent off a football field for swearing at the referee. You can be penalised on a tennis court for swearing at the umpire. You can be sent back down to the cells for swearing at a judge or a magistrate. But for most people profane swearing is a relatively harmless habit in which a man's everyday speech is peppered with expletives of one kind or another, often, alas, misusing the name of God or Christ. The Jewish commentary is right, of course, but it does not say all that needs to be said and the Commandment is capable of a much wider interpretation.

I had an interesting experience of this recently when lecturing in Israel to a mixed audience of Jews and Christians. I used the divine name and I was reminded kindly by one of the audience afterwards that that is something an orthodox Jew would never do. Hebrew people have always attached quite extraordinary significance to the name of Jahwe. That is reflected in the story of Jacob just before his meeting with Esau when Jacob said to the being who wrestled with him at the ford,

> Please tell me your name. But he replied, "Why do you ask my name?" Then he blessed him there.
> So Jacob called the place Peniel, saying, It is because I saw God face to face, and yet my life was spared.
>
> (Genesis 32: 29–30)

There is another important allusion to it in Exodus.

> But Moses said to God, Suppose I go to the Israelites and say to them, "The God of your fathers has sent me to you," and they ask me, "What is his name?" Then what shall I tell them?
> God said to Moses, Say to the Israelites, "The Lord, the God of your fathers – the God of Abraham, the God of Isaac and the God of Jacob – has sent me to you." This is my name for ever, the name by which I am to be remembered from generation to generation.
>
> (Exodus 3: 13–15)

Bishop Spong, in his book *The Living Commandments*, says that the phrase 'the Name of the Lord,' appears in the Old Testament seven hundred and fifty times and in the Psalms alone ninety-eight times. Now I normally do my own research, but Bishop Spong has done it before me and I take his word for it. As he says, 'To the Hebrew mind, the name of the Lord was holy and powerful . . . A name was not only a title; the name itself had mystery, power and substance. It was a handle on the very being of the person.' There is a good case, therefore, for saying that the commandment at its simplest level was simply a prohibition of the careless use of the name of Jahwe. Indeed, the Hebrews were so careful about the use of the name that they never used it at all and by a curious device used an entirely different name in worship and in public speech to avoid any possibility of using the original name carelessly.

One can only compare this reverence for the name of God with our lack of reverence for the name of God in common speech. Profanity for many people is just a tiresome habit but there is a sense in which it seriously devalues the currency and robs the name of its 'mystery, power and substance'. For many people the name of God is simply part of the everyday arsenal of invective.

The second possibility is that it is a prohibition of the use of the name for magical purposes. Magic was an ever present threat to the purity of the Hebrew faith, not only in Canaan itself, but throughout the cities of the ancient world where magicians, sorcerers and spiritists abounded. The knowledge of a sacred name initiated you into certain sacred mysteries. The knowledge of a sacred name gave you powers over other people which could be invoked to create disorder of mind or disease of body. The ancient world went in terror of spells which could destroy your crop, terminate your pregnancy, create delusions, cause you to lose a war.

In the light of this ask yourself why a Christian document about the life of Christ (St. Matthew) should give so much space to the visit of the wise men from the East. The word translated wise men there is 'Magi', who were so named because of their devotion to and skill in the practice of magic. There is no easy answer to that question.

You may have heard many sermons on the subject which do not even allude to it, but the most obvious answer is that St. Matthew was concerned to show that the practitioners of those ancient arts, in the persons of the three wise men, were submitting themselves to the sovereignty of Christ. It was an important message for the early Christians who, like their Jewish contemporaries, had to live in a world dominated by magic and had every reason to fear the power of magic over themselves. The child in the manger and the man on the cross, and ultimately the man in the Easter garden, was their only resource. Not only were they not themselves to take the name of the Lord their God in vain but they were not to be afraid of those who did.

So far I have made use of the term 'the ancient world' as if somehow we in the twentieth century were utterly remote from it. But one of the alarming features of the twentieth century has been the revival of magic, or its accompanying arts, in the minds of well educated, sophisticated, scientifically trained men and women. Recently there have been examples of it in the States, with deadly results. We have had our examples of it in Britain with the revival of witchcraft and popular astrology and the use of ouija boards. The problem is that the Angel of Darkness can often present himself as an Angel of Light and the genuine seeker after truth is often the most vulnerable subject.

Two men came to see me last year, both of them well educated, who told me of the devastating effects upon them and upon their families of a chance association with a group which professed to initiate them into the mysteries of life but was itself much more closely associated with magic than with religion. They took the trouble to come to see me because having only barely escaped from it themselves they were anxious that I should take some steps to warn other people (especially young people) against the solicitations of this particular cult.

The popular astrology which appears in the press might of itself seem harmless enough, especially as the advice is couched in such terms as to permit a wide variety of interpretations so that the astrologer must sometimes get his prophecies right. Indeed many people read them more for amusement than for edification, but they do read them, and their minds may be more dominated than they sometimes think in the course of the subsequent week by what they read in the astrologer's column on the Sunday.

It could be that the prophets so unceasingly spoke against magic in their day because they viewed it as an infringement of the third Commandment and for them the importance of the third Commandment was that it prohibited any action which either intentionally or unintentionally gave the impression that we had God in our pockets, that we could invoke His name for magical purposes, that we could make our own fortune and destroy someone else's by using the name as part of an incantation.

The world did not come to a halt at the end of B.C. and begin again at the beginning of A.D. The same forces which dominated the ancient world can easily dominate the modern world. The superstitions which we think we have summarily dismissed may invade us again in a different form and under a different name.

Do not be too sure that we are wiser than our fathers. Christ has won the victory over the spiritual forces of evil in heavenly places and we need to be on our guard against spiritual forces of evil on earth. Be careful not to misuse the name of the Lord your God.

In the Authorized Version the injunction was against taking the name of God in vain. The word translated 'in vain' means empty, groundless, insubstantial, unreal. That is why the Jewish Commentary, under the heading of the third Commandment, says –

> it forbids us to dishonour God by invoking His name, to attest what is untrue or by joining His name to anything frivolous or insincere.

But that does not confine the Commandment simply to the chance use of the name Jahwe. The Jews were a covenant people, enjoying a peculiar relationship with Jahwe, for whom *everything* that was done was considered to be done in the name of Jahwe and under His tutelage.

The Jews were, and always have been, a very humorous people and there are many flashes of humour which enliven the pages of the Sacred Scriptures themselves.

But they were never frivolous people. They have seen too much, suffered too much, agonised too much to be able to do anything but take a serious view of human life and its activities. The world is God's world and life has to be lived seriously, with a proper respect for the name of the God who presides over the destinies of the world.

Now we cannot acquire that experience, we can only reflect on the consequences of it and learn to take more seriously than we sometimes do this third Commandment – 'You shall not misuse the name of the Lord your God.' Christians, by grace, are now members

48

of the covenant people; they have assumed heavy responsibilities, they are instruments of God's purpose in the world and, even when they may never mention His name, their style of life will suggest to those around them whether they do or do not dishonour the name of God. Our Lord said:

> Do not swear at all; either by heaven, for it is God's throne; or by earth, for it is His footstool; or by Jerusalem, for it is the city of the Great King. And do not swear by your head, for you cannot make even one hair white or black. Simply let your "Yes" be "Yes", and your "No", "No"; anything beyond this comes from the evil one.
>
> (Matthew 5:34–37)

The saying may well not be original to our Lord at all and His hearers could well have recognised it as a quotation from the writings of the Jewish fathers.

Now let it be admitted that that injunction would severely limit our powers of conversation, and if you have ever sat next to someone at a dinner who simply said yes or no, you will know what I mean. But the intention is clear, although expressed in an extravagant form.

Even more than in our Lord's day, we live in a world dominated by, at the best, useless and, at the worst, misleading conversation – those endless 'chat' shows on the radio or television, those subtle circumlocutions in Congress or in Parliament, that spurious learning which has nothing much in view but the reputation of him who pretends to it, those exhausting cocktail parties in which we have to shout louder and louder to say less and less. The air, and even outer space, is full of conversation which yields little in the way of information and nothing in the way of truth.

There was a certain much-revered bishop of the Church of England who was well known for his dislike of social occasions. Having been very reluctantly persuaded to go to a wedding reception he greeted the first person he met with the words — 'How long is this dreadful occasion likely to last?' Unfortunately it was to the bride's mother that he was speaking.

Some of us will know the feeling only too well as it is expressed by George MacDonald in his *Diary of an Old Soul*:

> Why is it that so often I return from social
> converse with a spirit worn,
> A lack, a disappointment — even a sting
> Of shame, as for some low, unworthy thing?

I myself return sometimes from such social converse with a sense of insubstantiality, emptiness, vanity. If you ever feel like that yourself, take it as an invitation to retreat into your inner chamber and be still, waiting upon God whose name is Holy, who presides over the destinies of the world and of the whole universe, who will not have His name dishonoured by talk for talk's sake, in insincere opinion, by accommodation to the standards of the world.

When confused by the strife of tongues, wearied with controversy or conversation, seek God in the secret place, take hold of the golden string and find your way to reality, and truth, and new life.

5 THE FOURTH COMMANDMENT

Remember the Sabbath day by keeping it holy.
(Exodus 20:7)

There is a charming verse by Kenneth Fearing which epitomises modern western man. It goes like this:

And wow he died as wow he lived,
Going whop to the office, and blooie
home to sleep and
biff got married and bam had children
and oof got fired.
Zowie did he live and zowie did he die.

Amusing, yes, a bit near the bone, but that is how many of us live – commuting across the Atlantic, washing down a sharp deal with a few gin and tonics, struggling to maintain last year's figures, rushing into marriage and unhappily rushing out of it again, worrying about our children's examination results, and when we do have a bit of time off, consuming it in exhausting pleasures. Kenneth Fearing was right, 'wow we die as wow we live.' I ask you to compare the kind of life that so many of us live with the calm and healing tone of the fourth Commandment as it is recorded in the book of Exodus.

Remember the Sabbath day by keeping it holy.

Six days you shall labour and do all your work, but the seventh day is a Sabbath to the Lord your God. On it you shall not do any work, nor your manservant or maidservant, nor your animals, nor the alien within your gates.

For in six days the Lord made the heavens and the earth, the sea and all that is in them, but he rested on the seventh day. Therefore, the Lord blessed the Sabbath day and made it holy.

(Exodus 20:8–11)

Perhaps of all the Commandments, this is the one we most need to hear in our busy restless lives. 'Restless' perhaps is the word which best describes the kind of lives we have made for ourselves in the twentieth century – restless in mind, restless in body, restless in spirit, afraid to be still. That may seem a strange judgement to those of us who have been brought up to think of the Commandments in negative terms and almost forgetting that the first five Commandments are, even when negative in form, positive in content. This is one of them. It is a command to rest, and we are law-breakers in God's sight just as much if we ignore this Commandment as if we ignore the Commandments not to kill, steal, commit adultery, or covet other people's goods.

No one who knows anything of Israel's history, or indeed has any acquaintance of Judaism in our own day, would doubt the importance of the Sabbath for the Jew. It was the subject of intense study by the Rabbis, it was an inescapable obligation for the Jewish family, and an integral part of their home life. We have to remember what many of us forget, and that is that most of the Hebrews for most of the time lived outside the confines of the Holy Land. They lived in very unholy cities of the oriental or Mediterranean world; they lived, traded with and worked with Gentiles, who had no knowledge of their law and little sympathy with their way of life.

One of the strangest aspects of their life, in the minds of their Gentile neighbours, was their strange observance of the Sabbath. The Jewish shopkeeper kept his shop closed when his Gentile neighbour was making a handsome profit. The Jewish farmer stopped work however propitious the weather for seedtime or harvest. The Jewish traveller stayed put when his companions continued their journey.

Materially the observance of the Sabbath put the Jew at a disadvantage. Who was going to employ a man, and there was a lot of unemployment about, who refused to work on Saturday? What recruiting sergeant was going to recruit a man who refused to fight, or even to polish his boots on a Saturday? And if a Gentile contemplated marriage to a Jewish woman (which did, of course, occasionally happen) how was he going to adapt himself to a household in which all labour stopped on a Saturday?

So the Sabbath, when Jews were living in isolated communities in the ancient world, was not simply a habit, it was a badge – a badge of identity, setting the Jew over against the habits of the nation and the city in which he dwelt. It was an embarrassment but it was also a strength. You can covet, commit adultery, steal, even worship other gods in secret, but not to observe the Sabbath was a public act which carried with it excommunication from the people of God.

You would, I think, be surprised if you were to look carefully at the Gospels and find the number of times in which the Sabbath is mentioned and the number of so-called Sabbath disputes in which Jesus was involved. The word occurs sixty times and there are at least six distinct occasions in which Jesus was involved in disputes about the Sabbath with the leaders of official Judaism. It is made quite clear by the evangelists that He observed the Sabbath day and indeed preached His first sermon in a synagogue on the Sabbath day. But, so it would seem, He harboured what appeared to the Pharisees to be cavalier attitudes to the highly complicated regulations which had been built up around the Sabbath. Certainly it was His attitude to the Sabbath which first aroused the suspicions of the Jewish hierarchy and contributed largely to their fierce opposition to Him. So both for the disciples of the Pharisees and for the disciples of Christ, the Sabbath was a highly emotive issue and remained so in the subsequent relations between the early Church and Judaism.

But you may well say – 'It may have been important for the Jews and for the early Christians. But of what conceivable importance can it be to us, in a Christian civilisation which, if it observes anything, observes Sunday rather than Saturday, the first day of the week rather than the last?'

According to the scriptures the Sabbath was instituted at Sinai, together with the other Commandments of the decalogue. But you need to know that other origins have been suggested. The one most widely canvassed is that the idea of a Sabbath arose in Babylon. After all, Abraham came from that part of the world and it is true that there is a similar word employed in Babylonian manuscripts for a particular day associated with the phases of the moon.

But there is no evidence that the Jews themselves lived by a lunar calendar and if you use one of those diaries which shows the phases of the moon you will see that they do not match up to our seven-day week. Moreover, the Babylonian 'sabbaths' were regarded as days of evil omen, not days of rest or rejoicing. But it is undoubtedly true that from time immemorial, the number seven and the seventh day have had a special significance for mankind.

The story of the wise men in the New Testament is sufficient to remind us that the stars played a great part in the wisdom of the East. It is certainly possible that the famous Tower of Babel was in part a temple and in part an observatory. It was built 'up to heaven' not just for the fun of it but to facilitate the studies of the astronomers of the day and to make the music of the spheres more audible.

Recent astronomical studies have supplied us with extra planets but the Babylonians knew only of five, plus the sun and the moon. As these planets were easily distinguishable from the stars, seven therefore became a kind of sacred number. Babylonian observatories were made seven storeys high, their State documents were sealed with seven seals; there are seven colours, seven musical notes, seven parts of the body and human lives were supposed to consist of seven-year periods. The English and French languages between them preserve the association of the seven days of the week with the planets, viz. Sunday (Sun), Lundi (Moon), Mardi (Mars), Mercredi (Mercury), Jeudi (Jupiter), Vendredi (Venus), Saturday (Saturn).

The Hebrews, therefore, did not invent the seven-day week, but the Commandment at Sinai gave the seventh day a significance which, as far as I know, is peculiar to the Hebrew people. Both in the Exodus and in the Deuteronomy versions of the Ten Commandments, the seventh day is to be a day of 'ceasing'. The reasons given are different. In Deuteronomy the Sabbath was instituted to enable the Hebrews to 'remember that they were slaves in Egypt and that the Lord their God had brought them out with a mighty hand and an outstretched arm' and for that reason the Lord their God commanded them to keep the Sabbath day. In Exodus it was because God rested from creation on the Sabbath day.

That difference need not puzzle us. All the Commandments have a certain 'history' in themselves and were interpreted in different ways at different times in Israel's history. Both these interpretations had something important to say to the Hebrews and they have something important to say to us.

The Christian Sunday had originally nothing to do with the Jewish Sabbath, it was more appropriately called 'the Lord's day', and commemorated His glorious resurrection from the dead. The early Jewish converts to the Christian faith would have observed their Jewish Sabbath as usual but on the following morning they would have gathered together for the Christian Eucharist to thank God for the resurrection.

When, as the result of the apostolic mission, the Church became predominantly Gentile, the Gentiles would not have observed the Jewish Sabbath but they would have met together on the first day of the week, like the Jewish Church in Palestine, to commemorate the resurrection. It could not have been very easy to do so if you were a slave in a rich man's house, and you were expected to have the breakfast ready on the table when he came down. But it was regarded as obligatory to attend the Eucharist nevertheless.

There were times when it was positively dangerous to do so. At certain periods in the Roman Empire the Christian Church was proscribed, and to be known as an adherent would certainly put your livelihood, your promotion, your freedom and occasionally even your life, at stake. After the so-called conversion of the Roman Empire of course the situation changed, and the ideas of thanksgiving and rejoicing which were associated with Christian celebration of the Eucharist gradually affected and transformed the life of society as a whole.

To attend the ceremonies of the Church you had to have a day off, and Sunday became for the whole world what it has been ever since, except when the French Republic in the first flush of enthusiasm sought to abolish it and substitute a ten-day week. Thank God the experiment failed. We have enough problems with seven days – what would we feel like after ten?

So we see that by a curiously roundabout way the ideas associated with the Jewish Sabbath were appropriated by Christian civilisation, and the interpretation given in the Exodus version of the Commandments became a feature of the Christian Sunday. In England we are always being told horror stories about the so-called Victorian Sunday – days devoted to painful inaction in which the children were condemned to spending all day in their Sunday best and in which adults abstained from even the most harmless pursuits. It was nothing but hymns and sacred songs and Bibles and boredom.

But I am not sure whether, even if by accident, the Victorians were not wiser than we are. At least they recognised the necessity of 'ceasing'. One of the things that alarms me about modern society, on both sides of the Atlantic, is the degree of strain under which people in responsible positions live.

The history of our Prime Ministers in the last century in England has been a history of men struggling against

57

nature, denied adequate rest, overexposed to publicity with no privacy and little opportunity of 'ceasing', except opportunities created by illness. The finger on the button is too often the trembling finger of the man who, without wishing it, is infringing the fourth Commandment. He has no opportunity to cease, and sadly he loses the ability to cease, even when he could. The end is, as Kenneth Fearing said, 'Wow he died as wow he lived', a sad broken man, reduced to rags by an impossible timetable.

Now you will know as well as I do that this experience is not confined to the mighty in the land. The whole climate of society makes it difficult even for its humblest members to cease. Even when they themselves do cease they are surrounded by the noisy and intrusive activities of others and invaded by the general air of restlessness.

The Sabbath is not just a religious observance, whether it be for Jews on Saturday or for Christians on Sunday. It is an attitude to life. As one Jewish writer has put it,

> The Sabbath planted a heaven in every Jewish home, filling it with long-expected and blissfully greeted peace, making each home a sanctuary, the father a priest and the mother who lights the Sabbath candles an angel of light.

I can testify to this from personal experience. Greatly daring, my wife and I, when we last visited Jerusalem, went to the Orthodox quarter, Mea Shearim, on Sabbath eve. The streets were full of women and children, enchantingly dressed, laughing and greeting each other in the cool of the evening. Their husbands were in the synagogue. The synagogue service over, the men came out to join their families, and together they went back home.

Within half an hour or so the streets were empty and in the darkness lighted candles began to shine behind the windows, the families were together and the Sabbath rest had begun. To attend that Sabbath meal anywhere in Jewry is a rare and precious privilege. I have experienced the truth that by it heaven is planted in the loyal Jewish home.

I must tell you an old Rabbinic story. The question is – 'How does God spend His day?' The answer is – 'He spends eight hours administering the Universe, eight hours reading the Torah and eight hours playing with Leviathan.' If God finds it necessary to have a break, can we do without it? If God finds it necessary to take a day off, can we afford not to do so? But let it be a day off not just for noisy and exhausting pleasures but let it be a day off for re-creation, for the contemplation of the marvellous world in which we live, for the thankful remembrance of our Creator, for the humble thanksgiving for Him who was dead and is alive and reigns for evermore.

I end with the words of a certain Dr. Simpson, in a pamphlet called *The Power of Stillness*, based on the text 'Be still, and know that I am God.'

> We cannot go through life strong and fresh on constant express trains, with ten minutes for lunch; but we must have quiet hours, secret places of the Most High, times of waiting upon the Lord, when we renew our strength, and learn to mount up on wings as eagles and then come back to run and not be weary, and to walk and not faint. The best thing about this stillness is that it gives God a chance to work. "He that is

entered into His rest hath ceased from his own
works, even as God did from His."

I cannot remember how this pamphlet came into my
hands but I carry it with me always. Dr. Simpson put the
end of a golden string in my hand. I have myself been a bit
slow winding it in but I believe it can lead me to heaven's
gate built in Jerusalem's wall. Make a Sabbath in your
life. Rest from your labours as God did; be still and know
that He is God.

6 THE FIFTH COMMANDMENT

Honour your father and your mother.

(Exodus 20:12)

I am speaking to a father incensed that his son should come to a smart reception for his business associates dressed in a T-shirt devoted to the latest cult hero and in tattered jeans. I am speaking to the mother past the childbearing age who reflects, rather ruefully, on the obvious physical charms of her daughter. I am speaking to the radical undergraduate who is almost afraid to go home because of the rows he knows will ensue with his bourgeois parents. I am speaking to the young married woman who finds her mother-in-law insufferable, and the young married man who finds his father-in-law a bore. I am speaking to the grandfather who is afraid that before he shuffles off his mortal coil he will be shuffled off to some grey elderly people's home on the edge of the town. I am speaking to the middle-aged man who has carved out for himself a brilliant career in the academic world, who finds it no longer possible to relate to his parents who never completed an 'O' level education. This is what we call in shorthand 'the generation gap'.

I well remember the day when one of my family took me on at billiards and reached a hundred before I was past the twenties. But he is a kindly lad and we had a game of table-tennis afterwards in which he knew that I was still, though barely, his superior.

That is how life is, and always has been. The father finds himself with a son who is stronger than he and brings home a bigger wage packet. The mother finds herself with a daughter more beautiful than she and perhaps even more competent.

It is true that this generation gap has been ruthlessly exploited for commercial reasons in our own day but it is certainly not new. There are obvious examples of it in the Old Testament. Who could forget the story of David and Absalom – the indulgent father and the ambitious son who rebels against him. David, burdened with guilt, collapses and uncharacteristically flees for his life and is only delivered by that ruthless adjutant of his, Joab, at the cost of Absalom's life. 'O my son Absalom! If only I had died instead of you.'

But the trouble was he had not taken sufficient trouble when Absalom was alive to set his son on the right path and Absalom had dishonoured his father. It is evident even in the life of the Son of Man, as recorded in the Gospels, that there was a certain tension between Our Lord's own vocation to the service of God and His mother's understandable concern for Him.

Over against these undisputed facts of human existence stands this undisputed command – honour your father and your mother. The Hebrew people were, of course, as exposed to these tensions as any other member of the human race. The Rabbis of the first century B.C. can be heard deploring the fact that the young men of their day were having their hair cut short, that they were going to the gymnasium, that they were acting in the theatre – in fact that the younger generation were going to the dogs. Modern Jewish literature is full of examples of this tension. Isaac Singer wrote in his novel

The Manor of the 'pious and conservative Jew' who is upset when he finds that his daughter has married a sceptic. Here is a passage from one of Harry Kemelman's 'Rabbi' books — *Wednesday the Rabbi got Wet.* A Jewish boy is speaking about his family situation —

> My father has a drugstore, and when I graduated from pharmacy college and passed my licensing exam, I went to work for him. We never really got along.
>
> He had old-fashioned ideas — even about running the store. Lots of stuff he wouldn't carry because he'd say it wasn't in keeping with the dignity of a pharmacy. Even the way you filled prescriptions, it had to be just so. Like where every pharmacy in town used plastic tubes for putting up pills, he still used glass bottles because he said the tubes weren't air-tight, although there are only a few pills like nitroglycerin that deteriorate in the air.

and so they quarrelled and the boy left home and became the prey of one charlatan religion after another.

Yes, the tensions are there all right in every human home, Jewish, Christian, Moslem, Hindu. But few would dispute the quite remarkable solidarity of Jewish family life down the ages. It was one of the wonders of the ancient world and was greatly admired by their pagan neighbours. When I was Bishop of Liverpool I used occasionally to visit Walton Prison which had, in those days, three thousand prisoners. It was so rare to have a Jewish boy in prison that the Governor would draw my attention to it. Perhaps it has something to do with the fifth Commandment; the command to honour your

63

father and your mother carried with it a certain reciprocity – parents could hardly expect to be 'honoured' if they did not themselves love and care for their children.

The Ten Commandments are customarily divided into two tables, the one relating to our duty to God and the other relating to our duty to our neighbour. Scholars are never quite sure to which table the fifth Commandment belongs. It might seem obvious that it belongs to the second table but there is something to be said for the argument that it really belongs to the first, and that duty to parents is part of our duty to God. And indeed the word for honour is a word used with equal frequency for the honouring of people and the honouring of God. The root word means heavy, weighty, substantial and in its verbal form it means to respect, to glory in, or to glorify. So close is this association with the glorifying of God that when this Commandment is quoted in Leviticus 19, verse 3, the Hebrew word translated honour is one otherwise exclusively used in relation to God. So it could be said that in honouring your father and mother you are honouring God, and the attitude to your parents inculcated from childhood can become the vehicle for a consuming love and reverence for God in your later years. The Commandment, therefore, stands on the border between our relationship with God and our relationship with our neighbours and it certainly meant much more to the Jew than simply an item in a humanitarian code of conduct.

It is significant that God revealed Himself to Moses as 'the God of Abraham, Isaac and Jacob' and that the phrase 'the God of your fathers' recurs so often in the sacred Scriptures. In origin the Commandment may well have had much more to do with ancestral religion than with care for the aged. To honour your father and your mother meant to accept the religion which they professed and taught. It was the vehicle by which the true religion of Jahwe was transmitted down the ages from Abraham, to Isaac, to Jacob, to Moses, to David, to Ezra, to Ruth, to Joseph, to Jesus. Every Jewish child was taught to say at the offering of the first fruits —

> My father was a wandering Aramean, and he went down into Egypt with a few people and lived there and became a great nation, powerful and numerous.
>
> (Deut. 26:5)

My favourite Jewish musical *Fiddler on the Roof* puts it this way — 'You ask me how we know these things. The answer is TRADITION.' That enormously influential tradition, nurtured amongst the Hebrew people and subsequently bestowed upon the Christian Church and upon all mankind, was preserved, in part at least, by the authority of the fifth Commandment — 'honour your father and your mother' and, as it implied, honour the religion they professed. It was not possible to honour your father and mother without honouring their God.

It constitutes a burdensome command, as we would see it, for the young and a heavy responsibility for the old. But we ought not just for those reasons to discard it. Tradition can indeed be a disastrous handicap to progress and those of us who belong to the Church know that full well. But in most walks of life it is indispensable.

I would hesitate to submit my body to a surgeon who despised the medical knowledge of the ages and proposed to operate solely on the basis of his own hunch. I would not expect to gain much from the philosopher who gloried in his ignorance of the philosophy of the ages. I would not expect to get a very good degree at university if my professor insisted on starting all over again without recourse to the great masters of the past. I would not be drawn to the latest fancy cult which has no roots in the history of the human race. We remain, for all our modernity, the children of Abraham, Isaac and Jacob, and we cannot, even if we would, start all over again.

The Commandment of course had social consequences as well as religious foundations and that is the significance of the words which follow immediately upon it, 'that you may live long in the land which the Lord your God is giving you'. This is not a promise of individual longevity. It is part of the covenant relationship between God and the people as a whole. Obedience to the commands of God was the condition under which the tribes of Israel were promised the land and it was the condition under which they remained in the land.

The prophets were never tired of saying that the promise was not unconditional and the later prophets explained the disasters that overtook Israel by insisting that it was due to their disavowal of the original covenant with God. So the solidarity of the human family, in which children honoured their parents, was an ingredient of the solidarity of society as a whole. This is how it is put by a Jewish commentator —

> The home is infinitely more important to a people than the schools, the professions or its political life; and filial respect is the ground of national permanence and prosperity. If a nation thinks of its past with contempt, it may well contemplate its future with despair.

66

That is plain speaking, but I go along with it. The relationships established in the home are the relationships which are carried out into society. The fractious home creates the fractious society. The home in which mercy and forgiveness are not known produces a society without pity for its weaker members. The home which is the seat of an incessant struggle for power is the mirror of a society in which power is sought for its own sake, without regard for those over whom that power is exercised. We have all been children, we have all had parents. What happens behind our smart front door does not just dispose us as a family to happiness or misery. It is either renewing or destroying the whole community to which we belong. The Jewish commentator was right, 'filial respect (and if we may add, paternal love) is the ground of national permanence and prosperity.'

The third principle enshrined in the fifth Commandment is what we might call the principle of authority. Of all the issues which trouble modern society this must be one of the most intransigent.

In his book *Dilemma of Democracy* Lord Hailsham, Lord Chancellor of England, has a chapter headed 'The City of Destruction' and this is a passage from it —

> I continue to believe in democracy and wish for more of it rather than less. But the evidence to the contrary is profoundly discouraging. Democracy has a very bad track record. Among forms of human government, it has been the rare exception and, where it has emerged, it has always seemed to carry within it the seeds of its own destruction. It has been short-lived. Even where it has not succumbed to external aggression, it has proved unable to withstand or

defend itself against pressures from within, the spendthrifts who disperse its resources, the class warriors who break up its unity, the separatists who try to divide it geographically, the lobbies and pressure groups who try to cajole, corrupt or intimidate its governments, the political parties who undo or undermine each other's activities.

'The City of Destruction' was a good title for the chapter and George Orwell may not have been so far out in his prospects for 1984. No society can survive without order, and no order is conceivable without some generally accepted principle of authority. The child honours (or is supposed to) his father and mother. The undergraduate (maybe) honours his professor. The shop steward (less likely) honours the managing director. The voter would like (genuinely so) to honour the man or woman he places in supreme power over the nation.

Our problems flow from an inadequate perception and an imperfect realisation of authority. The fifth Commandment is an expression of that principle of authority in a domestic and tribal situation. The honour which a child is expected to give to his parents was based on the authority which the parents were presumed to have received from God Himself. They were God's agents in bringing up God's children. They, no doubt very imperfectly, reflected the honour and glory of God and that is why the word honour can be used of our relationships with human beings or with God.

The principle of authority is part and parcel of the whole order of creation. God spoke and the world was made. God commanded the waters of the Red Sea and they parted. The great universe itself moves at God's command. We live under the absolute, overwhelming authority of the God of all creation and that authority is refracted, however imperfectly, in the miniature authorities we exercise on earth.

I end with a most revealing passage from the pages of the New Testament:

> When Jesus had entered Capernaum, a centurion came to him, asking for help. "Lord," he said, "my servant lies at home paralysed and in terrible suffering."
>
> Jesus said, "I will go and heal him."
>
> The centurion replied, "Lord, I do not deserve to have you come under my roof. But just say the word, and my servant will be healed. For I myself am a man under authority, with soldiers under me. I tell this one, 'Go', and he goes; and that one, 'Come', and he comes. I say to my servant, 'Do this,' and he does it."
>
> When Jesus heard this, he was astonished and said to those following him, "I tell you the truth, I have not found anyone in Israel with such faith."
>
> (Matthew 8:5–10)

The centurion, as he rightly observed, was able to order his men about, not because there was anything special about him but because he served one greater than himself, the great Emperor in Rome. His uniform, his rank, represented the ruler of the whole inhabited world. He was quick to see that Our Lord's authority was of the same kind. There was no need for Him to come to his house, He could command and it would be done. And why? Because Our Lord Himself was acting with the authority of the great King in heaven, Master of the world, Ruler of the universe.

This was an astonishing insight for a Gentile soldier, as Our Lord recognised. The fifth Commandment is, or could be, the end of a golden string, in so far as when it is taken seriously it leads on to a conception of universal authority to which we bow, or in the end perish. Fathers and mothers, statesmen and generals, professors and archbishops, exercise authority. There can be no ordered society, whether political or ecclesiastical, in which the principle of authority is ignored. But those who, for better or for worse, exercise authority had better see to it that they do so in humble reverence for God, the source and spring of all authority.

7 THE SIXTH COMMANDMENT

You shall not murder.

(Exodus 20:13)

I have a copy of Ambrose Bierce's famous *Devil's Dictionary*, to which I often refer. It abounds with sardonic definitions of familiar words. I particularly like his definition of optimist – 'the man who looks on the bright side of other people's troubles'. And pessimist – 'the man who has to live with him'. I like too his definition of an egoist – 'a person of low taste, more interested in himself than me'. Or mausoleum – 'the final and funniest folly of the rich'. Yes, and he has a definition of the decalogue – 'a series of commandments, ten in number, just enough to permit an intelligent selection for observance but not enough to embarrass the choice'. But the Biblical scholar would have to say to Ambrose Bierce, in all seriousness, that there is no question of choice. The individual commandments were all part of a relationship without which God's covenant with Israel was null and void. They were not prescriptions for a happy social life, they were the conditions under which the Chosen People were to live if they were to remain Chosen. They were, to use technical language, part of the covenant. They do not permit, to use Ambrose Bierce's words, 'an intelligent selection for observance', *all* have to be attempted.

71

I have now come to the end of what is sometimes called the First Table of the Commandments, primarily concerned with our duties to God, and am now beginning on the Second Table of Commandments, commonly thought to be concerned with our duties to men. But this distinction will not stand. I have been surprised to discover how dominant a part the relationship with God plays in the decalogue. After all, we are now half way through and we have not even begun to think about human conduct as such. We have been exclusively concerned with our attitudes to God and His absolute claim upon our lives.

But even when we move on to what is called the Second Table we do not leave the First Table behind. Commandments six to ten arise directly out of Commandments one to five. This is an important point so may I illustrate it? We are commanded not to commit murder. Why? Most of us would say that it is because any kind of humane social life is impossible where people take the law into their own hands, or where human life is cheap. But to the Hebrew mind the reason is that it is God who has given us life and men are not allowed to take it away. The next Commandment, not to commit adultery, is not simply concerned with creating a stable home life and protecting children from the consequences of its disruption. It represents a fundamental feature of our relationship with God. The prophet Hosea married a prostitute, or at least married a woman who subsequently became a prostitute, and this personal experience became a vehicle for him to expound one of the great truths of the Bible, i.e. that God is faithful, despite our apostasies. Faithfulness is part of God's relationship to us and this has to be reflected in faithfulness to our fellow human beings.

We are not to steal. Why? Because we have been conditioned by living in a bourgeois society to value individual property? Or is it simply a device used by the rich to protect themselves against the poor? Or is it of no significance anyway, because we are all insured up to the hilt and may indeed profit from the occasional burglary? The answer, to the Hebrew mind is that the possession of property is a stake in God's world and every man is entitled to just that element of security. Strangers and pilgrims on the earth indeed we are, homeless in the universe, but most of us can only tolerate that condition when God in His mercy provides us with some slight inheritance on earth.

I remember my own sense of relief when, some five years ago, my wife and I actually bought a house for our retirement. After all, Bishopthorpe Palace, for all its grandeur and its distinctive place amongst the great houses of England, is, as far as we are concerned, a 'tied cottage'. We are only strangers and pilgrims in it. We pass on.

In one country parish I know two estates were built. One by the local Council for renting, the other for private purchase. They were both built by the same builder. Within a matter of weeks it was not difficult to tell which was which. The one remained brightly painted, well decorated, with trim gardens and well cut lawns, on the other the gates were hanging off their hinges, broken window panes were not replaced, grass was growing up through the flagstones. Why should this be so? It was not a question of wealth or practical ability, it was a question of whether the house belonged to somebody or whether it did not.

That is one of the reasons I suppose why the Jewish people retain a fanatical devotion to the land of their origins. It represents for them a stake in God's kingdom on earth. So the command not to steal derives from a total world view.

The ninth Commandment tells us not to bear false witness. False witness is not just an affront to a judicial system or a denial of the human rights of another person but an affront to God. This is the basis of that rather mysterious verse in St. Paul's second letter to the Corinthians:

> For no matter how many promises God has made, they are "Yes" in Christ. And so through him the "Amen" is spoken by us to the glory of God.
>
> (2 Corinth. 1:20)

The word 'Amen' is a derivative from the word meaning truth. The whole created order depends upon the reliability of God, who is Himself the truth. To bear false witness is not just to endanger another man's life or his freedom but to compromise our understanding of the principles upon which the universe is built.

And why are we not to covet? Because God has given us all things richly to enjoy, and we had better get on enjoying them rather than coveting the things that other people happen to be enjoying.

I hope you are convinced that you cannot separate the second set of Commandments from the first. That is to say you cannot build an ethical system on the Ten Commandments without regard to their origin in the mind of God and in the Chosen People's understanding of their role in the world. Atheist or agnostic philosophers are perfectly entitled to build suitable ethical systems but they cannot claim the Ten Commandments given at Sinai in support of them. The decalogue is about God and our relationship with Him through our relationships with others. St. John put it very succinctly —

> anyone who does not love his brother whom he
> has seen, cannot love God whom he has not seen.
> (1 John 4:20)

And now to the sixth Commandment in particular. You will have got used to the notion by now that things are never as simple as they seem. The older English versions translated the Hebrew word — 'thou shalt not *kill*'. If indeed it did mean just that it was manifestly disobeyed by the Hebrews themselves, who killed a lot of people (for example in their conquest of Canaan) and acquired a reputation in the ancient world for the utmost ferocity. Throughout their history members of the race were in great demand as mercenary soldiers and at one stage Egypt employed a mercenary army of some 30,000 Jews to guard their northern frontier. We have seen a revival of their military skills in this century.

The Hebrews did not have any scruples about capital punishment. They interpreted it in a slightly different way from ourselves but they had no hesitation in employing it. Those who breached the Covenant paid the price with their own lives. So the phrase 'thou shalt not kill' is not sufficiently distinct to be useful. That is why the New International Version prefers 'you shall not murder.' Thus it moves the issue away from the mere act of taking life, whether in war or in self-defence, to the motive behind it. And this is true to Hebrew tradition.

The word translated 'kill' is relatively unusual in the Old Testament in comparison with other words also

75

meaning to kill. Gradually over the years it acquired a certain kind of 'inwardness' where everything depended upon the motive rather than the act. This development reaches its consummation in the words of Jesus in the New Testament,

> You have heard that it was said to the people long ago, "Do not murder, and anyone who murders will be subject to judgment." But I tell you that anyone who is angry with his brother will be subject to judgment. Again, anyone who says to his brother "Raca" is answerable to the Sanhedrin. But anyone who says, "You fool!" will be in danger of the fire of hell.
>
> (Matthew 5:21–22)

When put this way the Commandment becomes uncomfortably comprehensive. Few of us will kill, but which one of us has never been angry with a parent, or a child, or a husband, or a wife, or another fellow human being. We are all in danger of the judgment, flames of hell are reaching up to us, we smell the fire, we anticipate the searing pain. But the meaning of the word is not exhausted in its personal or individual aspects. There is a kind of destructive anger which can go along with the domestic virtues, with charm of manner and friendliness, with humanitarianism of the highest degree. But we can still murder people.

You will no doubt have wondered, as I have, why it should be that the world so devoted to peace in principle should be so violent in practice. The causes of violence are sometimes, of course, obvious enough – gross inequality between races, gross exploitation of the poor by the rich, the desire for power at any price and the pressure of a growing population on scarce resources. But some of the violence we experience is not even as respectable as that. It appears to be without aim, meaning or cause.

Anyone who has followed in the trail of the supporters of an unsuccessful 'away' side cannot but be horrified at the violence and the damage which is caused. The fact that your side has lost 2-nil away from home cannot of itself really account for such a trail of broken glass and broken ads. Or why, as in a recent case in England, should a group of young people torment, torture and ultimately murder an old lady in her flat. She was poor, there was nothing to steal, she was quite unknown to the intruders, she had not provoked them – but she died in a pool of blood. Or why should a man conceive of violent hatred of clergymen. He killed the first in Ramsgate, he killed the second in Scotland and was about to kill the third in York when he was apprehended. All we clergy, I can tell you, kept our doors shut whilst he was on the rampage.

This kind of motiveless, mindless violence takes a lot of explaining and some psychologists explain it with the word 'rage'. It is more than 'anger' which might well be provoked. It erupts from the inner volcano of a man's life and issues in murder. It covers much of our contemporary society with an ugly black volcanic slag.

This kind of rage may take three forms; it could well take more forms than that, but these are the three that occur to me. Sometimes it represents a kind of rage against society. It is true that on the whole society is divided between 'the winners' and 'the losers'. The winners do not always win on their own merits, the losers do not always lose because of their own faults, but the losers who know they are losers can easily be trapped in a kind of irrational rage which expresses itself not simply on the football terraces or in the streets but in their own attitudes of mind. Some make war on society deliberately (the criminals, the anarchists), others just opt out and buy a croft in some out of the way place on a distant moor where they suppose they are immune to society. But whatever form it takes it proceeds from a kind of anger, a rage against society.

The same can be said of a rather different kind of rage, although not easy to distinguish in practice, and that is a rage against life itself. It is expressed in Holy Scripture in the book of Job, who rages against the kind of life in which the innocent suffer and the wicked triumph. It sometimes takes the form of a loathing of nature as in Sartre's book *La Nausee*. Here is a quotation from it:

> I remember better what I felt the other day on the sea-shore when I was holding that pebble. It was a sort of sweet disgust. How unpleasant it was! And it came from the pebble, I'm sure of that, it passed from the pebble into my hands. Yes, that's it, that's exactly it: a sort of nausea in the hands. Underneath the hard outline (he says of the root of a chestnut tree) is only a kind of shapeless, senseless mass.

Commonly it rails against the seeming meaninglessness of all existence as, for example, in Kafka's novels.

Sometimes – and this is a third form rage can take – it is rage against God himself. In the Sixties in England, and I've no doubt in the Sixties in America as well, a series of writers arose who contributed to what came to be known as 'Death of God Theology'. It was a pantechnicon term covering a wide variety of use and of course meaningless

78

in itself. If God was ever alive he could not now be dead. If God is now dead he could never have been alive. In some cases the writer has meant no more than that the familiar categories in which faith is expressed no longer mean anything to most of the inhabitants of this earth. And who would quarrel with that judgement.

But for some it meant more. It was a rage against the ultimate being, an expression of total despair. We were the inhabitants of a universe which ultimately descends into a 'black hole'. Therefore the so-called 'creator' of the universe is to be hated and despised. God may indeed not be dead, but they wanted him to be dead; after all humanity did crucify the Lord of Glory on a little hill outside Jerusalem and this modern song which I now quote represents that feeling very vividly.

FRIDAY MORNING

It was on a Friday morning
That they took me from the cell,
And I saw they had a carpenter
To crucify as well.
You can blame it on to Pilate
You can blame it on the Jews,
You can blame it on the Devil,
It's God I accuse.
It's God they ought to crucify
Instead of you and me,
I said to the carpenter
A-hanging on the tree.

You can blame it on to Adam,
You can blame it on to Eve.
You can blame it on the apple,
But that I can't believe.
It was God that made the Devil
And the Woman and the Man,
And there wouldn't be an Apple
If it wasn't in the plan.
It's God they ought to crucify
Instead of you and me,
I said to the carpenter
A-hanging on the tree.

He that is angry with his brother is in danger of the judgement, our Lord said, and that is the ultimate refinement of a review of life which had its origin in the sixth Commandment — 'You shall not murder.' But where, we may well ask, amidst all this darkness and violence and self-destructiveness, is the end of a golden string which can lead us to Jerusalem's gate?

There is a word in the New Testament which stands over against all anger, or rage, or violence, or self-destructiveness. It is not benevolence which is how we would tend to put it, but peace. 'My peace,' Jesus said to His disciples, 'I give to you.' It is a rich word both in its Hebrew and Greek forms. In the Hebrew form it is Shalom. In its Greek form it is Eirene. It means much more than absence of war. It means well-being on the basis of a wholesome relationship with God and a wholesome relationship with our fellow beings.

But we have to observe that it is a *gift*. It is not the end product of a long process of culture or self-discipline, it cannot be achieved or won. Hence those other strange words — 'my peace I give unto you.' Jesus was, so we believe, the living embodiment of a proper wholesome relationship with God and an unfailingly loving relationship with other men. It is this peace that he gives us, we share in his Shalom; we find ourselves at unity with the creator, with the creation, and with all created beings. Here indeed is the end of a golden string, in a labyrinthine world in which we wander hopelessly at the mercy of our own and other people's anger. It is said of that marvellous Quaker saint, John Woolman, that he loved the slaves but he loved the slave owners too. Would-be reformers of society could well take a leaf out of his book; they too, will need to accept for themselves, in Christ, the gift of peace.

8 THE SEVENTH COMMANDMENT

You shall not commit adultery.

(Exodus 20:14)

Arthur Clough, an English author of the nineteenth century, had his own sardonic version of the Commandments and here is part of it —

Thou shalt not kill; but need'st not strive
Officiously to keep alive.

Do not adultery commit;
Advantage rarely comes of it.

Thou shalt not steal; an empty feat,
When it's so lucrative to cheat.

Thou shalt not covet; but tradition
Approves all forms of competition.

Arthur Clough was right — 'advantage rarely comes of it'. It is a costly sin in terms of social and personal disorder. The divorce rate in the States is worse than ours in England but ours is bad enough. In 1950 the number of Decrees Absolute granted was just short of 29,000 in Britain. By the middle of the 1970s that figure had risen to 138,000. In 1950 there were 209,000 divorced people in Britain. By 1977 this figure had reached 1,370,000, i.e. over a million people who are bearing the burden and bitterness of divorce.

But even worse is the number of children under sixteen who are put at risk by the divorce proceedings of their parents. In 1970 this number was 71,000; by 1977 the number had risen to 154,000. Every policeman, every school teacher, every minister of the Gospel, every probation officer, would say that there is a connection between the growth of delinquency, childhood stress, truancy and the rise in the divorce rate. The cost to society in terms of social disruption and of government spending on divorce is immense.

Now of course not all divorce petitions are filed on the basis of the adultery of one of the partners. In fact, a friend of mine who is an experienced marriage guidance counsellor says that a surprisingly large proportion of marital difficulties arise from misunderstandings about money. That could well be so, but it remains true that it is often an act of adultery, or the suspicion of adultery, which finally disrupts the marriage. It is a potent and furtive destroyer of home life and every year puts thousands more children at risk. Clough was right — 'advantage rarely comes of it', however attractive, romantic, exciting it may seem at the time. But the cost borne in terms of human suffering is infinitely more significant than what we might call the statistical cost to society as a whole.

My wife and I were returning from the far west of Wales after a holiday in an old Morris car which crawled over the Prescelly mountains and finally came to a grinding halt in a town at the other side. So there was nothing for it but to stay the night and we had to make do with a friendly, but not very attractive, hotel in the main street. We were there on our own, apart from a youngish man in his thirties and three children.

We could hardly fail to take particular note of them and could not help hearing their conversation. It was an obvious case of a man, divorced from his wife, with the children in her custody, paying his monthly visit to the old marital home and taking the children out for a treat.

So there he was, trying to come to terms with the children whom he only saw under highly artificial conditions once a month, children who were bewildered at the course of events in which they were involved and were obviously deeply embarrassed by this monthly 'treat'. His jollity was rather forced, their response very muted. God knows what they made of it all, and what the effects were going to be on their own attitudes to marriage and home life.

A friend of ours whose husband went off with another woman, and who subsequently had to take divorce proceedings, told me of the shame and despair she felt every time she had to fill in a form which required that she describe her marital status. 'Divorced' she wrote, with trembling hand and downcast eyes. Of course, divorce no longer carries the social stigma that it did, but it was not social stigma that she was worried about; it was the sense of being deserted, unwanted, cast off.

I have been speaking about adultery in these precise terms because the original Commandment, 'You shall not commit adultery' was interpreted in precise terms and the word has a distinct meaning. With some possible exceptions it meant sexual intercourse of a man with another man's wife, and the law was that both the man and woman were to be put to death. This in itself was a measure of the seriousness with which the offence was taken. In the book of Job, Chapter 24, verses 14 and 15 it is regarded as on a par with murder, and the prohibition has in view the protection of home life and the sanctity of marriage. That is one of the reasons why Jewish home life, even when lived in a pagan environment, was one of the wonders of the ancient world, and why still, in Britain at least, so few Jewish children appear in court or Jewish youths appear in jail.

The prohibition was carried over into the early Church and into the New Testament as St. Paul said —

> The acts of the sinful nature are obvious: sexual immorality, impurity and debauchery; idolatry and witchcraft; hatred, discord, jealousy, fits of rage, selfish ambition, dissensions, factions and envy; drunkenness, orgies, and the like.
> I warn you, as I did before, that those who live like this will not inherit the kingdom of God.
>
> (Galatians 5:19–21)

It may be of some comfort to us to know that the early Christians were not paragons of virtue. This letter was written to a Christian congregation and I have to say that I have never, as Bishop or Archbishop, ever had to write to a Christian congregation in these terms. So the moral standards of the early Church may have been high but they were not universally observed.

But notice two things about this list, apart from its comprehensiveness. First observe that those who are guilty of these things will not inherit the kingdom of God, that is to say there are certain things — attitudes, actions, aspirations — which exclude people from a loving relationship with God, which is our proper inheritance. Second, notice how what we might call sins of the flesh appear in the list next to sins of quite a different kind, one of which is idolatry. It is this which partly accounts for the seriousness with which the Hebrew people viewed the sin of adultery. But adultery was not simply an offence against another person, or even an offence against society, it was an offence against God, the God of Israel, the God of Abraham, Isaac and Jacob who, so they believed, was the author of the Commandments.

There is one prophet who brings this out with painful clarity as a result of his own experience, and that prophet is Hosea. Scholars have long discussed the nature of the marriage relationship with his wife which lies at the heart of the book. They ask – 'Was Gomer a prostitute when he married her or did she become a prostitute after he had married her?' Whatever the answer to that question, was she just a prostitute in the ordinary 'street' sense or was she a temple prostitute, associated with the fertility rites which dominated the Canaanite religion of the day?

If she was a temple prostitute then it is easy to see how adultery comes to be associated with idolatry or apostasy. The prophet Hosea certainly saw the connection himself because he used the sad story of his own marriage to illustrate the gross adultery of Israel with foreign gods, thus betraying their relationship with the one true God. Hosea's own marriage, and the adultery of his wife, became the burden of his own prophetic message.

It is in that sense a heart-rending book, showing how a man's own bitter and painful experience of desertion became the vehicle of one of the greatest revelations made to us in the pages of the Old Testament. And the revelation is this, that adultery betrays a precious human relationship and destroys it and, by the same token, adultery with other gods, unbelief and apostasy, betray a proper relationship between Israel and Jahwe. Adultery represents faithlessness in human relationships on a par with faithlessness in a man's relationship with God.

It is the mark of Hosea's greatness that his experience with Gomer fortified him in his relationship with God rather than destroyed him, but alas, for many others that is not so. Their experience of faithlessness on the part of the marriage partner serves only to instil in them an attitude of distrust, suspicion and guardedness in all their relationships with other people and may make it indeed difficult for them to believe in God at all. The man who goes off with another woman does not simply destroy his marriage and ruin his children, he may make it impossible for any of those affected by his action to develop loving relationships with other men or with God.

One of the most painful pastoral episodes in which I have ever been involved concerned the case of a woman who, after a long period of mental illness, was certified insane and removed to hospital. She was, according to the best medical opinion, incurable and by the law of the time such a person could be divorced by the marriage partner because she was in no position to look after her home or her children or her husband – and never would be. So the husband got a divorce, married again and together with his new wife lived in the old home.

But his previous wife, against all expectations, got better and was discharged from hospital and looked forward to resuming the old life with her husband, wholly unaware that her marriage had been dissolved. I have never had a more difficult case to deal with. No one could blame the husband for what he had done; he had not committed adultery, he had not broken the law, he was doing what he thought best for himself and his family. But for his first wife it was devastating. Her glowing hopes of the future disappeared like a morning cloud, the dream of getting better turned into a nightmare. Life for her was a black hole into which she just disappeared.

Living faith in God was the only answer, but living faith in God was the one thing she was not capable of. What, to her, seemed her husband's faithlessness spoke to her of the faithlessness of God. The Hebrews were right, there is a close connection between adultery and faithlessness.

I compare that episode with others of a much happier kind. One of the most moving moments in the life of a minister of the Gospel is to stand at the chancel step and officiate at the marriage of a young couple, glowing with hope and vitality, confident of the future, charmed with each other.

But there is an even more moving moment than that and that is to celebrate the service of Holy Communion with two elderly people and their friends rejoicing in their Golden Wedding Anniversary — fifty years later. Of course they have had their problems, of course there were moments when they wished they might never have met each other, of course they have experienced distance from each other and even antagonism, but through it all they remained faithful. There was something in those lined faces which was even more beautiful than in the fresh and joyous faces with which they had first made their vows to each other.

Faithfulness is a huge virtue in human affairs but one which is often little regarded. If you have to choose between an attractive romance (or so it seems) and faithfulness, for God's sake choose faithfulness.

But I speak now to those who have experienced marriage breakdown and now find themselves writing in the appropriate column of every form they have to fill in 'divorced'. Are they barred, as St. Paul suggested, from the kingdom of God? Is the gate to Eden for ever shut against them? Is there any golden string I can put into their hand?

Our Lord's attitude to such situations was, at the same time, more penetrating and more merciful than was common amongst the religious teachers of His day. On the one hand, He vastly extends the concept of adultery beyond the act of sexual intercourse with a married woman.

> You have heard that it was said, "Do not commit adultery." But I tell you that anyone who looks at a woman lustfully has already committed adultery with her in his heart.
>
> (Matthew 5:27–28)

That must make some of us less confident than we might suppose in our eternal salvation, for what man or woman in the world has not sometimes been guilty of that. But perhaps the most telling illustration of His attitude is contained in a passage from St. John's Gospel which is almost certainly not part of the original text, but there is no reason to doubt its authenticity within the general traditions about Jesus's ministry.

> Jesus went to the Mount of Olives. At dawn he appeared again in the temple courts where all the people gathered around him, and he sat down to teach them. The teachers of the law and the Pharisees brought in a woman caught in adultery. They made her stand before the group and said to Jesus, "Teacher, this woman was caught in the act of adultery. In the Law Moses commanded us to stone such women. Now what

do you say?" They were using this question as a trap, in order to have a basis for accusing him.

But Jesus bent down and started to write on the ground with his finger. When they kept on questioning him, he straightened up and said to them, "If any one of you is without sin, let him be the first to throw a stone at her." Again he stooped down and wrote on the ground.

At this, those who heard began to go away one at a time, the oldest ones first, until only Jesus was left with the woman still standing there.' Jesus straightened up and asked her, "Woman, where are your accusers? Has no one condemned you?"

"No one, sir," she continued.

"Then neither do I condemn you," declared Jesus. "Go now and leave your life of sin."

(John 8:1–11)

The woman was actually taken in the act of adultery and there was no doubt about her guilt and no doubt either about the sentence — 'Moses in the law commanded that such should be stoned.' His answer to her accusers is in line with His words in the Sermon on the Mount — 'If anyone of you is without sin, let him be the first to throw a stone at her.' No one did, either amongst the old men or the young, because as they knew full well, each one of them had been guilty of adultery in the heart if not in the bed.

And then in a single phrase Jesus releases the woman from her past — 'Neither do I condemn you', and at the same time emphasises the extreme gravity of what she had done — 'Go now and leave your life of sin.' Not only had she escaped physical death, she now had the opportunity of escaping spiritual death as well. The door to the kingdom of Heaven was open if she cared to walk through.

The Christian Church has often emphasised the sins of the flesh out of all proportion to the sins for which our Lord reserved his most extreme judgements – the sins of pride, arrogance, indifference, bigotry. It is possible, alas, to be an upright, pure, sexually-continent, well-respected man and yet to have the harlots and the publicans go into the kingdom ahead of you. We are all in the same position before the throne of God. If we have not been faithless to our wives we may have been faithless to others and we may well have been faithless to God. Old or young, wise or foolish, religious or irreligious, respectable or criminal, we all have need of that golden string which will lead us in at Heaven's gate. Genuine repentance and the grateful acceptance of Christ's forgiveness is the only way for us, as it was for the woman taken in adultery.

9 THE EIGHTH COMMANDMENT

You shall not steal.

(Exodus 20:15)

On Thursday, August 8th, 1963 a train set out from Glasgow for London carrying, amongst other things, two and a half million pounds worth of Treasury Notes destined for the Bank of England. Some hours later, at a rather unexpected point on the route as far as the engine driver was concerned, he was held up by a red signal. Within a matter of seconds the footplate had been taken over by armed men wearing masks and Balaclava helmets; within a matter of minutes the men in the mail van, which was immediately behind the engine, had been overpowered and the train was under the control of the famous 'Train Robbers'. Both the engine and the mail van were detached from the rest of the train and driven off. It was quite a long time before a puzzled guard walked up the line to see what had happened, found himself without an engine, a mail van or a driver, and set off in the utmost bewilderment to raise the alarm.

The police were soon on the scene and roadblocks were established in the surrounding countryside. But the robbers got clean away with two and a half million pounds worth of Treasury Notes, the largest haul in the history of British crime.

They had, of course, anticipated the roadblocks and

had, several months before, purchased a derelict and isolated farmhouse not far from the scene of the robbery in which they intended to hide out until the roads were clear again. It was an audacious, well conceived, carefully planned scheme and was called by the press the 'perfect crime', but like so many well conceived plans it was ruined by a simple oversight on the part of one of the gang. The farmhouse was tracked down by the police long after the gang had left but one of the members of the gang who had been made responsible for removing all signs of fingerprints had failed to do so.

Within hours the police records had identified every single man involved in the robbery. Within months most of them were behind bars. Some of them almost gave themselves up, trapped in the tightening net which the police had wrapped around them and impoverished (believe it or not) by the blackmailing of other members of the underworld who were in the know. When the organiser of the robbery himself was arrested he delivered himself of the heartfelt conviction, perhaps a little delayed, that 'crime doesn't pay.' But that is not why I am telling you the story. I do so for another reason and it is this – to comment on the strange reaction of the British public to this crime.

The robbery was the subject of intense speculation, but what was more interesting was the ambivalent attitude towards it, expressed both in private conversation and in the mass media. There was a certain grudging admiration for the skill and audacity of the operation and also a certain feeling that it didn't matter anyway because it was only the Bank of England that had lost the money. Indeed, several films reconstructing the events were made and avidly watched in cinemas and on television and in a recent book on the subsequent history of the train robbers they are described as folk heroes, squalid and fruitless though their lives proved to be. They were the Robin Hoods of the 20th century.

It was, of course, regrettable that the engine driver was so seriously injured in the affray that he was permanently disabled and lost his means of livelihood, and it was true, of course, that the manipulation of the signals which made the robbery possible could have caused a massive pile-up on the railway with the loss of many lives. But the money, so it was felt, didn't really belong to anybody and nobody was the loser except the insurance company which had taken on the risk. Indeed, the kind of qualities of daring which the robbers had exhibited were the qualities which in a different age would have made them pioneers and empire builders.

What emerges in the end from this tale is that we are less clear than our forefathers were about our moral attitudes to theft. On the whole, it is agreed that murder is a bad thing and adultery (if it is someone else's) is a threat to family life and social cohesion. But theft does not always carry with it nowadays moral censure as it did for the Hebrews and we must ask ourselves why.

There are several possible answers to this question. First is the growing awareness of the sometimes very fine distinction between criminal and legal activity. As Clough said in his satirical revision of the Commandments,

> Thou shalt not steal; an empty feat,
> When it's so lucrative to cheat.

Why bother in fact with a complicated and dangerous operation robbing a train when you can make a killing on the Stock Exchange and win yourself half a million or more without actually breaking the law at all? Why dress yourself up with a mask and a Balaclava helmet when you can walk to the office in a neat pin-striped suit, bowler hat and an umbrella and rob society of millions with a well-timed take-over bid? Why run the risk of injuring or killing an engine driver and robbing him of his livelihood when you can rob thousands of their livelihood by disposing of an industry in the interests of profit? Why spend the best years of your life behind bars when you can spend the best years of your life living it up in a prosperous suburb, popular with your friends, honoured in the Honours List and receive a gold watch when you retire by manipulating the money market to your own advantage? So it comes about that robbery of the old fashioned sort does not seem so heinous as one might suppose.

The second answer is more far-reaching in its implication, and it is to this that I shall devote most of the rest of this chapter. Whatever may have been the failures of Marxism in creating a credible social system, it has been marvellously successful in implanting in the Western mind a deep suspicion of property as such. Proudhon, a Marxist theorist of the nineteenth century, who coined the phrase 'scientific socialism' also delivered himself of the famous aphorism – 'property is theft'. That phrase, which does not mean exactly what it seems to mean, is now an accepted part of Marxist dogma, as well established in human minds as the Ten Commandments themselves. If property is theft it can be no crime to steal other people's property.

With this I ask you to compare the Hebrew attitude to property, as it is reflected in the Commandment itself and in the legislation both civil and criminal which is attached to it. A standard Jewish Commentary, to which I often refer, has a sub-title to the eighth Commandment and it is this – 'the sanctity of property'.

The reasons for this emphasis are not far to seek. Relations in the ancient world were much more direct than they are in ours; furthermore, property was, for many people, their only means of livelihood. If someone breaks into your house and steals your television set and your tape recorder and your jewellery, you still survive. If on the other hand someone steals your flocks and drives away your cattle, you will not survive. There were no banks, no insurance companies. If you were a nomad, as the Hebrews were for part of their national history, you had no mattress to hide your money in, no secret cache to which you could return at a later date. Theft could destroy you, or at least impoverish you for ever.

We have to remember too the point which I have made before, that the second table of Commandments does not constitute a simple system of ethics; it is an expression of a relationship with God, and the eighth Commandment is no exception. Property, in the Hebrew view, was a gift of God; it gave you a stake in God's creation; it offered you a patch of land to which you could devote your life's work; it enabled you to plant vineyards to ensure the survival of your family or your clan. Therefore, not even a king had the right to appropriate one of his subject's properties. Here is the classic statement of a citizen's right to resist 'compulsory purchase':

> Sometime later there was an incident involving a vineyard belonging to Naboth the Jezreelite. The vineyard was in Jezreel, close to the palace of Ahab, king of Samaria. Ahab said to Naboth, "Let me have your vineyard to use for a vegetable garden since it is close to my palace.

In exchange I will give you a better vineyard or, if you prefer, I will pay you whatever it is worth."

But Naboth replied, "The Lord forbid that I should give you the inheritance of my fathers."

So Ahab went home, sullen and angry because Naboth the Jezreelite had said, "I will not give you the inheritance of my fathers." He lay on his bed sulking and refused to eat.

(1 Kings 21:1–4)

Left to himself, Ahab might have remained sullen but he was sufficiently aware of the law of God not to have pressed his claim any further. His wife Jezebel, a foreign princess, who owed no loyalty to the law of Israel, thought otherwise and said:

Is this how you act as king over Israel? Get up and eat! Cheer up. I'll get you the vineyard of Naboth the Jezreelite.

(1 Kings 21:7)

So she engineered a false charge against Naboth, called false witnesses and had him stoned to death, and Ahab went down to the vineyard to take possession of it.

Elijah, the prophet, was in no doubt about the heinousness of the crime which Ahab had committed.

Say to him, "This is what the Lord says: Have you not murdered a man and seized his property?" Then say to him, "This is what the Lord says: In the place where dogs licked up Naboth's blood, dogs will lick up your blood-yes, yours!"

(1 Kings 21:19)

Observe how carefully murder and theft are associated in the prophet's mind, and wonder in your heart at the amazing sense of the righteousness of God which lies behind the Commandment not to steal.

Well, you may say, we now live in a much more complex society than that and things are no longer just black and white. In England the law still stands over against the executive and can still preserve a private citizen's right of property. If you ever travel on the trans-Pennines motorway you will reach a point where that great motorway divides. And why does it divide? Because the farmer over whose land the road was taken resisted a Compulsory Purchase Order on his farmhouse and insisted on staying in it. His appeal was upheld by the legislature, so he still sits there, marooned but proud, in front of the hearth before which his forefathers sat, with the traffic thundering past on each side.

'Quixotic' you may say, but it stands for an important principle which we neglect at our peril. The possession of property is not a sin. Property is not theft. It represents a stake in God's world; it imposes responsibilities as well as conferring privileges. It gives a man a sense of belonging to the earth which God made. It is rightly understood to be a sacrament of God's providence.

So-called 'public ownership' is no substitute for it. I own the Gas Board and the coal mines and British Rail and the steel industry, in so far as they are in public ownership — but I have no control over them. I do not share in their successes and thank God I am not responsible for their failures.

But I do own a house for my retirement in a pretty village in Oxfordshire and it is my pride and joy to work in the garden, and then to sit on the garden seat and view my achievements. A society which proceeds on

Proudhon's dictum that 'property is theft' and substitutes for it universal public ownership does not, in practice, seem to create either a happy or a prosperous community.

I derive a certain cynical amusement from reading year after year with monotonous regularity about the failures of agriculture in the USSR. The weather has been too hot, or too cold, too wet or too dry. They have tractors but no spares, and even farming machinery as large as combine harvesters get lost on obscure railway sidings far from the corn fields for which they were destined. And so it comes about that the Soviet Union with a huge land area still depends upon the capitalistic, property-owning West for its supplies of grain.

Why? It cannot be just the weather, or just the soil; it has something to do with the attitude of those who work the land. It is said that the acre or two which individual farm workers are allowed to cultivate in the Soviet Union produce nearly as much as the enormous acreage under communal control. There is a story which used to circulate in the Soviet Union which went as follows. When the farmhand was awakened to be told that the cows were calving, he replied – 'they are the people's cows, let the people look after them.'

The Christian attitude to property at first glance seems ambivalent. On the one hand it has never condemned ownership and has never embraced Utopianism. On the other hand it retains within its tradition, as recorded in the New Testament, some very striking sayings of our Lord which seem to challenge the whole concept of property, e.g. Luke 12:15 'a man's life does not consist of the abundance of the things he possesses', and Matthew 19:24 'It is easier for a camel to go through the eye of a needle than for a rich man to enter the kingdom of Heaven.' And there is the classic statement of the theme in the discussion with a young man who, when invited to become a disciple, went sorrowfully away – for he had great possessions.

Indeed, the early monastic movements in the Christian Church could lay claim to such texts in their insistence on poverty, or to put it another way, lack of ownership, as one of the vows which a monk must take. Yet some of the monasteries ultimately became sickeningly rich, owning huge tracts of country and often employing labour for minimum wages. The folk lore of monasticism abounds in examples of men who genuinely renounced wealth and ownership only to become possessively attached to the little things they did own or use – the cell in which they lived, the place at which they sat in Chapel or in the refectory and the love of little private possessions by which they established their identity in the community.

Nevertheless, we shall have to say that it is difficult for a rich man to enter the kingdom of Heaven, it is difficult for someone with great possessions to follow Christ with undivided mind, it is difficult for a prosperous society to sacrifice itself in the interests of a less prosperous society, it is difficult for the Western nations to retain their hold on Christian faith and, at the same time, to deny the claims of the Third World. For most of us this issue arises at some time or another in however subtle a form.

I live in a big house by the river Ouse, three miles south of York. I do not own it, in the fullness of time I shall be leaving it to someone else. But it could easily give me grand ideas, it could easily make me dissatisfied with the little place in which I shall subsequently live, it could blur the edges of my commitment, it could soften my mind, my body and my spirit. *The* Son of Man had nowhere to lay his head, He was a pilgrim and a stranger on the earth, His only personal possession a robe for which they cast lots at His crucifixion. He was dependent on others for the bare necessities of life. He was *the* Son of Man but He summons many another son of man to follow Him. Happy is the son of man who does not go sorrowfully away because he has great possessions.

I offer you this end of a golden string from a poem by Amy Carmichael, founder of the Dohnavur Fellowship in Tinnevelly, South India, which challenges much more in our attitudes to life than mere possession of property.

> From prayer that asks that I may be
> Sheltered from winds that beat on Thee,
> From fearing when I should aspire,
> From faltering when I should climb higher,
> From silken self, O Captain, free
> Thy soldier who would follow Thee.
>
> From subtle love of softening things,
> From easy choices, weakenings,
> Not thus are spirits fortified,
> Not this way went the Crucified,
> From all that dims Thy Calvary,
> O Lamb of God, deliver me.

10 THE NINTH COMMANDMENT

You shall not give false testimony against your neighbour.

(Exodus 20:16)

The picture conjured up in our minds by this Commandment is of the witness in the box testifying that he is about to speak the truth, the whole truth and nothing but the truth, so help him God. There is no doubt that the original Commandment had some such specific meaning, although we would have to be cautious about the use of the word 'perjury' because it is by no means clear that it was customary for the ancient Hebrews to give evidence under oath. Nevertheless, to give false testimony was a very serious offence, and rightly so, because a man's freedom and even his life could depend on it.

There is a striking example of the consequences of false testimony in the famous story of Naboth's vineyard, already referred to where Jezebel arranged for witnesses to be suborned in order to accomplish Naboth's conviction and death. Another example, more familiar to the readers of the New Testament, is concerned with Jesus's trial, where every attempt was made to procure those who would falsify their testimony.

Christian scholars are apt to say that the Commandment relates only to false testimony against a neighbour, that is to say, a member of the Covenant people. Modern Jewish scholars deny that it can be so limited – and I think with some reason. Moreover, they extend the range of the Commandment far beyond the law court, and I quote from a Jewish commentary:

> the prohibition embraces all forms of slander, defamation, and misrepresentation, whether of an individual, a group, a people, a race or a faith.

So we are in the presence of a far-reaching Commandment which can be legitimately applied to a whole range of human activity in which the truth is set over against the lie, in which integrity is set over against insincerity, in which information is set over against propaganda, and in which facts are set over against rumours.

I know of no other place in which this issue is set out in bleaker form than in George Orwell's famous book *Nineteen Eighty-Four*.

> The Ministry of Truth was startlingly different from any other object in sight. It was an enormous pyramidal structure of glittering white concrete, soaring up, terrace after terrace, 300 metres into the air. From where Winston stood it was just possible to read, picked out on its white face in elegant lettering, the three slogans of the Party:

> WAR IS PEACE
> FREEDOM IS SLAVERY
> IGNORANCE IS STRENGTH

Most of us are agreed that lying is a bad thing. Even in a world in which other moral standards have shifted, the schoolboy who lies to his teacher, the man who lies to his wife, the director who lies to his fellow-directors, the managing director who lies to the shareholders, or the boss who lies to his employees is still regarded with extreme disfavour. It is one of the curiosities of English public life that a Member of Parliament can get away with almost anything provided he does not lie about it in the House. That, in parliamentary terms, is the unforgivable sin. A man's political career will seldom survive it. It is not difficult to see why, because lying strikes at the root of all personal or social relationships. It breeds distrust, it imperils friendships, it makes honest commercial transactions impossible, and it creates a miasma of falsity which clouds the fairest day.

Lying of this individual kind usually proceeds from cowardice or an unwillingness to face up to facts; it is sometimes the consequence of a long process of self-deception, as damaging to the person who lies as it is to those who are affected by the lies. We live in a world now where the lie is not just a hasty response to an unwelcome situation but an instrument of policy; George Orwell's description of the Ministry of Truth represents the culmination of a process of deception which has reached terrifying proportions already in our society. In many fields of human activity we have already reached 1984 and George Orwell's predictions have become alarmingly real. May I offer you a few examples of the ways in which the ninth Commandment 'You shall not give false testimony' is regularly and deliberately infringed.

The first casualty, they say, of any war is the truth, and both sides are invariably guilty of it. The past master of the art of lying was Dr. Goebbels of the Ministry of Information in Nazi Germany. In his hands it became an art form and no one would doubt that it contributed enormously to the triumph of the Nazi movement in Germany itself and the early successes of Germany in the Second World War. Up to the very end he was still talking about victories on the Russian front, the implacable determination of the Fuehrer and the security of the Fatherland even when the Russian artillery was within twenty miles of Berlin, the allied forces were closing in from the west and the Fuehrer was little more than a gibbering lunatic, trapped in his bunker in Berlin. But no nation at war, so it would seem, can dispense with the lie as an instrument of policy – the stream of denunciations of atrocities, the false hopes raised by a trifling victory, the reassuring noises about new instruments of defence to a panic-stricken population.

There is a sense in which lying propaganda is, in the eyes of the majority of us, wholly justifiable and the deceiving of the enemy is a worthy cause. There is no doubt that the defeat of the fascist powers in the Second World War owed a good deal to subtle deceptions at which, so it would seem, the English were particularly good. Some of you may be familiar with the book or the film entitled *The Man Who Never Was* – the story of how a dead man was dressed in a uniform, given a documentary history, provided with a passport and launched from a submarine in the Mediterranean, with documents which ultimately led the German High Command to move powerful forces from a front which was under attack to a front against which no attack was contemplated. It was a brilliant, if bizarre, example of successful deception and I cannot find it in my heart personally to regret it.

But the machinery of propaganda and deception, sedulously cultivated in the time of war, is not easy to dismantle; when people come to read of it thirty or forty years later, as we are doing now, you begin to wonder whether similar deceptions are being practised in our own day, not any longer in pursuit of war but perhaps in pursuit of political power.

My dictionary illustrates an interesting progression in the meaning of the word 'propaganda'. It meant originally, of course, simply to propagate, as you would propagate seedlings or plants. Then it came to mean 'the congregation or committee of Cardinals for the propagation of a faith', and then 'an organised method and system of propagating or disseminating principles and doctrines'. Now it nearly always means 'propagating or disseminating misleading principles and doctrines'. Our newspapers and weekly reviews are full of propaganda which, even when true in substance, may be handled in such a way as to mislead or to win support for some cause or other.

Then consider the whole field of what is called investigative journalism. This is not conducted in a court of law under rigid rules of evidence, it is conducted by men whose primary interest is in news, and in the selling of newspapers. Insinuations may well be made just on the right side of the law to avoid libel action, to which the victim is wholly unable to reply. Elaborate plots are uncovered which exist nowhere but in the fecund imagination of the investigative journalist.

Watergate is a striking example in our own day of successful investigative journalism and few would be disposed to condemn it – the truth was there waiting to be uncovered.

But alas we have had some cases in England where that is by no means the case. Solemn committees of inquiry have been set up to investigate allegations and in more than one case the whole edifice of accusation has crumbled into the dust, leaving the instigators no doubt chastened but the victims ruined. Men are apt to remember the accusations and to forget the acquittal. Character assassination is part and parcel of political life everywhere and we have all heard of the 'dirty tricks brigade' who, without actually making accusations, insinuate thoughts into the mind of the electorate which create an aura of suspicion around the unfortunate candidate. If he denies it he publicises it, if he ignores it he implies that he has no defence against it. The man who has false testimony given against him is in no position to defend himself. He cannot win.

Now I propose to tread in a mine-field where many rash travellers have already been blown to pieces. I refer to the world of advertising, a world incidentally in which I have many virtuous, well-intentioned and wholly honest friends. It is, so we are told, the essential engine for any commercial society. It promotes consumption, builds up the manufacturing industries, keeps people in employment and tells the customer what he needs to know. Yet I find myself, with many others, unhappy about it.

Some years back a member of my family spent six months or so in a kibbutz in Israel as a volunteer. He had many adjustments to make when he returned home, as one would expect. He was never a starry-eyed idealist and he was aware of the same processes at work in a kibbutz as are at work in every level of society. He never proposed to become a kibbutznik.

But the one thing which hit him as he got off the plane at Heathrow, travelled by tube to London and mounted to the surface on those endless escalators, was the advertising – that marvellous after-shave lotion which would attract a retinue of adoring women, those sexy stockings which men could hardly resist looking at, that particular brand of cigarettes which inevitably marked out the truly masculine or the truly elegant user, that brewery advertisement which pictured its particular chain of public houses as centres of light and warmth and good cheer, that patent medicine which was to be the elixir of life, that car which was to be a paragon of reliability and the envy of your friends, and that breakfast food which pops and sparkles in the morning sun at the breakfast table.

These advertisements were, of course, grossly misleading. The car may be back in the garage three weeks after you have purchased it, most of the pubs in that particular chain could be squalid, disagreeable places in which shady deals were made and petty crime plotted. And the after-shave lotion may wholly fail to attract a retinue of beautiful women.

But far more serious than the fact that these advertisements are misleading is what is implied by them. The ideals they represent to the public, even if they are attainable, are not worth attaining. They represent life as a triviality and persistently set before people objectives which are ludicrously inadequate. Put it in this crude way – even if the products are everything they are said to be, they are not worth having. I hasten to say that I am not blaming the advertising industry; I am simply commenting on the quality of a society in which a brilliant advertising industry is called upon to perpetuate ideals and objectives so thin and so insubstantial. We have created for ourselves an artificial world and we are unconsciously corrupted by it.

Truth is more than the simple absence of lies, and lies are not the only means of deception. I shall always remember one wise man's remark that for success in the world today you need the qualities that in a previous generation would have made a man a confidence trickster or a bigamist. There are just too many people about in the 'charm business'. They appear on public platforms, they fill our television screens, and they impose themselves upon us in the cinema or the theatre. It is calculated charm, designed to please and to attract, bearing no relation to the real man. In fact the real man disappears altogether and the entertainer of this kind ends up by scarcely knowing who he is.

But such characters are not confined, alas, to the stage or the television screen, or the fun show. We are all at risk. What about the image you project at the cocktail party? What about the man you purport to be at the trade union meeting? How does the man standing at the bar in the club compare with the man who puts out the light and goes upstairs to bed? How does the breezy man-of-the-world really feel when confronted with the news of a terminal illness? In short, does how we appear relate in any meaningful sense to what we really are? Every day of our lives we give false testimony about ourselves and we infringe the law of God.

Is there any end of a golden string at which we can clutch in a world so dominated by misinformation and false ideals, in which we share and to which we contribute by our own self-deceptions and insincerities? The word 'truth' is often on our Lord's lips and especially so as His life and teaching are recorded in St. John's Gospel. On the whole He uses the word 'truth' not in contrast to lies but in opposition to falsehood at a deeper level, viz. unreality, insincerity.

The fact of the matter is that we do not always set out to deceive; we do not really know who we are and therefore we project an identity which varies with circumstances and with the company we happen to be keeping at the time. We are not just culpable of untruth, we are simply incapable of truth. We have many faces and we play many parts. We are actors, stereotypes, caricatures, and we have difficulty in distinguishing one part from another. We start playing Hamlet and find ourselves playing King Lear; we thought we were playing a bassoon and find we are playing a piccolo.

The story is told of a soldier in the Second World War who was blown up by a mine and badly shocked. He had no documents and he could not remember who he was. And so he was put on a platform in front of the unit to which he was presumed to have belonged but no one recognised him. The same process was repeated before several other units to which he could have belonged. Nobody recognised him. And then came the agonising cry – 'Cannot anyone tell me who I am?'

Our Lord described Himself in one passage as the Way, the Truth and the Life. When I first began to read the Gospels in the RAF during the Second World War I emerged from this experience with one unshaken conviction which has been with me ever since – if this man is not true then nothing is true. After many years now of study and reflection and ministry I rejoice in the same conviction. It does not mean that He knew the whole truth about everything. It does mean that He was a complete, unified, and whole person, not trying to create an impression, not adapting Himself to make circumstances easy or to avoid difficulty, not living at different levels, but a man always the same. He was unchanging in His devotion to God and His compassion for men, without pretence or affectation, neither currying favour nor deliberately provoking confrontation; the same man at a party or at a funeral, the same man on the hills of His beloved Galilee or in the Garden of Gethsemane, the same man on the Mount of Transfiguration and lifted on the Cross at Calvary, the same man whom Mary Magdalen loved on earth and whom she continued to love in Heaven, the same man whom Peter trusted in his ministry to the Galileans and in his subsequent ministry to the Samaritans, to the Gentiles and to the nations of the earth. This man was the Truth.

When Paul uttered those extraordinary words, 'For me to live is Christ' he was giving expression to at least part of his experience. He had found his true self in Christ.

11 THE TENTH COMMANDMENT

> You shall not covet your neighbour's house. You
> shall not covet your neighbour's wife, or his
> manservant or maidservant, his ox or donkey, or
> anything that belongs to your neighbour.
>
> (Exodus 20:17)

Western society has given itself various names
over the last twenty years. There was the 'affluent' society
which mirrored the optimism and the confidence of the
booming years of the late 1950's. This was soon altered
to the 'effluent' society as the problems consequent upon
economic growth were more vividly seen – the pollution
of our rivers, the destruction of our lakes, poisoning of
the land and of the air, and the effect of exhaust fumes on
the city dweller. As a reaction came the 'responsible'
society which exalted the virtues of the so-called
'responsible' citizen called to play his part in the forming
of society and of the 'responsible' nation prepared to
sacrifice its own immediate interests to the feeding and
healing of the Third World. Then we have had the
'consumer' society, perhaps the most horrifying thing
that could be said of any society which appears to live by
the consumption of goods and things and food. More
recently in England we have grown familiar with the
'caring' society, i.e. that society which exhibits the
characteristics surely certified by the Gospel caring

for those unable to care for themselves, weighting decision in favour of the under-privileged, concentrating resources where they are most needed rather than where they are most profitable, for example in hospitals, in prisons, youth clubs and clinics.

But perhaps there is one adjective which could have been applied to our society throughout the last twenty years and possibly throughout the last two hundred years. For whatever else we may have been, we have remained fairly consistently a 'covetous' society dominated as we have been by notions of profit, of personal advantage at the expense of others, treating luxuries as if they were necessities, penetrated through and through by envy or 'differentials' as we tend to describe it, taking more than our fair share of the world's resources, blithely indifferent to the effects of our covetousness upon posterity. It is not enough to say as Groucho Marx said, 'What has posterity ever done for me?' We have been blatantly ignoring the tenth Commandment—

> You shall not covet your neighbour's house. You shall not covet your neighbour's wife, or his manservant or maidservant, his ox or donkey, or anything that belongs to your neighbour.
> (Exodus 20:17)

You shall not try to keep up with the Jones's; you shall not cast a lustful eye on the attractive young wife next door; you shall not envy your boss's Cadillac; you shall not plot a take-over bid of the firm down the road; you shall not exploit the rich mineral resources of another nation without regard to that nation's economy; you shall not lie in wait for the lonely walker in the subway.

114

The list could be expanded indefinitely; the Commandment covers pretty well every aspect of life that you can think of and it arraigns Western society at the judgement seat of the God of Sinai, uttering His voice and that a mighty voice, three thousand five hundred years ago to the people of Israel. We have no excuse. The Commandment is clear and the consequences of ignoring it are everywhere to be seen.

Try to imagine a society in which covetousness was not the moving principle. Inflation for example is not just an economic matter, painful though the economic consequences can be. It is a moral matter. Put simply, so the expert tells us, it is caused by 'too much money pursuing too few goods' i.e. it springs out of a desire for more and more which inevitably puts the prices up.

It is a moral matter also in the sense that it tends to undermine confidence in the future, it makes people extravagant; it makes future provision for your own family a waste of effort and it excludes whole ranges of our population from the necessities of life, whilst others indulge themselves in the luxuries. It creates bitterness between the classes and magnifies the differences between the rich and the poor. Inflation indeed is not just an economic matter to be alternately restricted or encouraged by economic policies. It strikes at the heart of any civilised society.

To take another example – we have had more than our fair share in Britain of industrial disputes. Some of them are not between labour and management but between rival unions wishing to preserve differentials, envious of the success of another branch of the industry, willing at any cost to destroy an industry rather than to see others profit equally from it. Some people call it collective bargaining, the Bible calls it covetousness. A High Court

115

judge last year, speaking to an international conference for young people held in York, commented on the tendency apparent in all Western countries for crime to increase with affluence. As a young man, he said, he looked forward to the day when full employment, education, good housing and adequate health provisions would reduce the crime rate in so far as there was nothing to be achieved by crime when people had all that they needed. Forty years on, he had to acknowledge that his confidence had been misplaced. Well educated men were engaging in organised crime. Men already rich were planning bigger and better bank robberies. Children who had everything they needed at home were stealing from supermarkets. Smooth operators in a cultural way of business were being convicted of elaborate and far-ranging frauds. Big companies already making huge profits were prepared to wink at corruption in order to make bigger profits.

The young people from Germany, Holland, France, the United States, from Israel, from Spain, from Brazil, from Norway and Denmark, from Kenya and the Sudan, from England, Scotland, Ireland and Wales, nodded their heads sagely. The High Court judge was right, of course. The statistics prove it up to the hilt. Why do people who have so much want more? Only God knows why, that is presumably why He committed to His people the tenth Commandment — 'You shall not covet.' If the Commandment were observed, we would not need policemen, we would not need courts, we would not need prisons or remand homes and we would not need High Court judges. If we did not covet, the toll of human misery would be greatly reduced.

Let me offer another example. Arthur Clough's version of the tenth Commandment is —

Thou shalt not covet; but tradition
Approves all forms of competition.

Competition is the spice of life. We get excited about an England/Australian Test Match and the FA Cup Final just as Americans do about the World Series and the Super Bowl. I am as eager to win in the squash court as any other man. The Olympic Games originated in a legitimate and health-giving form of competition and we owe the Greeks a great debt for it.

Under a Conservative Government in Britain we are now committed to the principle of competition, reducing the State monopolies, breaking up the cartels, selling off nationalised industries to private bidders and encouraging the salesman to go out and get the orders. I would not presume to offer examples from the United States but I take it that the competition principle is firmly entrenched in this great nation. 'Tradition approves all forms of competition.' We shall have to say that tradition may approve of them but some of them constitute blatant disobedience to the tenth Commandment.

I will tell you now a true story which you may find difficult to believe. In an urban borough in England there was a certain narrowing in the road which led to a disproportionate number of motor accidents, and the nearby hospital was kept busy dealing with the results of them. The Borough Council felt under some obligation therefore to discuss the issue. The cost of widening the road, which would have had to include the purchase of some of the front gardens of the adjoining houses, was going to be high and there would obviously be a powerful lobby of protest from the householders concerned. It was going to be difficult to get it through the finance committee. So the accountants were instructed to engage

117

in a costing exercise. They were to produce figures which would show on the one hand how much it would cost to widen the road and on the other how much it would cost to provide extra facilities at the local hospital – and to enlarge the nearby mortuary. Now, of course, these worthy councillors did not make their decision on the basis of simple cost effectiveness. Nevertheless, in order to give their decisions respectability they had to prove that it was 'profitable' to widen the road.

Profit is a perfectly legitimate means of assessing efficiency and keeping down costs, of improving techniques, and excluding waste. It constitutes part of our faith in competition. But I think most of you will agree that the profit principle could hardly be legitimately applied to the case I have described. On that particular balance sheet, the cost of widening the road ought not to have been set against the cost of improving the facilities at the hospital, but against the cost of death, disability, pain, grief and mental suffering.

But we must not take refuge in blaming the government, or blaming the local council or blaming society as a whole. Who cannot but be aware of the coveting principle within himself.

My camera is old, but perfectly adequate. I can take bad photographs on this one as well as I can take them on any other. But on my way to the chemists, I pass a camera shop and I look in the windows at those new, glossy, sophisticated little machines and I have visions of photographs of blinding clarity and beauty.

On my way back I pass the same shop. Now, one particular model catches my eye. It is the very latest thing. So I think it will not do any harm if I go into the shop and have a look at it – just a matter of interest, you know. It is obvious to me that I cannot afford it and that I do not need it, so I resist temptation and I go home. But three days later I need to go to the Post Office and once more I pass the same shop. Once more I look at the same camera. And now it begins to dawn on me that my old camera is really grossly inefficient, that it is no wonder that I produce photographs which are too light or too dark, which are seldom in focus, which have a habit of leaving my subjects without a head or any feet. It begins to be obvious that I need to have a new camera, that I am just wasting expensive film on the old one and that indeed it would in the end be 'profitable' to spend £60 on this glossy new model.

By the next day it is obvious to me that I cannot live without it, that it is a necessity of life.

Have you ever detected yourself in the same exercise? The coveting principle runs very deep in the human heart and we have ourselves to blame for it, not the government. It is the individual not just the nation which clamours for more than his fair share of the world's resources, which treats luxuries as necessities, exploits the earth for his own satisfaction.

Perhaps this is the point at which we ought to cease from our own self-examination and look at the Commandment itself. At first sight it seems strangely out of place in the decalogue. You can be convicted of murder, adultery can lead to a court case, you can be arrested for stealing and you can be imprisoned for giving false evidence, but you can hardly be tried for coveting. No policeman on duty near the camera shop is going to tap me on the shoulder and take me into custody for coveting the camera. He would only do so if I broke the window and snatched it.

What, then, is this Commandment doing here, describing a state of mind rather than an action? A good deal of scholarly endeavour has been poured into this problem, but the oddity remains. By no sleight of hand, as far as I can see, can the tenth Commandment be regarded as an indictable offence, nor indeed can it be catered for within any legislative system. But perhaps this highlights a feature of the Ten Commandments to which I have alluded before but which can easily be overlooked. What I have said about the tenth Commandment could well be said of some of the others. There is no penalty prescribed for making a carved image in the secrecy of your own home. There is no means of knowing whether in your own heart you worship the one true God or whether you worship others. It is not easy as a matter of conscience to know whether you are honouring your father or mother or not. For all the importance of the Sabbath observance in Judaism a man may work mentally as hard as he likes without risk either of arrest or even excommunication. Far more than we sometimes imagine the Commandments are concerned with inner attitudes of mind not just with actions or words. In the famous story of Naboth's vineyard, Ahab's downfall began when he coveted that vineyard. He was a rich man already. He had plenty of land and he could no doubt easily have bought more land if he really needed it but he 'coveted' Naboth's vineyard. The whole process of tragic events involving false witness, theft, murder, death, political defeat, and national disturbance was set in train by an inward state of mind which the king did nothing to resist.

May I illustrate this in another way, in a way which may appeal to those of you who are married or contemplating marriage? In the early stages of a relationship it is what a man says which makes an impression. How could it be otherwise? You have no other means of judging. Somewhat later in their relationship it is what a man does which makes the difference. But in the end, what makes or mars a marriage is what a man *is*. He may say nice things at breakfast or more likely at bedtime; he may invariably remember the wedding anniversary and give you nice presents; he may *do* all the right things and be a good, respectable citizen and yet what he is makes him impossible to live with. The Bible everywhere concentrates on what people are, not just on what they do or what they say.

Therefore Jesus was only reviving an ancient tradition when He insisted on the inner application of the Ten Commandments. A man may resist overt adultery and yet be guilty before God of covert adultery. A man may not commit murder but he commits murder in his heart when he is angry with his brother. In a curious way therefore the Commandments do cohere. The first one is concerned with our attitude to God which is not a matter capable of judgement by other people. The last Commandment is concerned with our attitude to people and to things which again are not subject to judgement by other people. In both cases we are on our own with God as indeed we always are in the deepest issues of life.

This is why Jesus's conversation with Nicodemus is so far-reaching in its implications. Nicodemus was 'a master in Israel' learned in the law, reverently acclaimed as a spiritual guide, a member of the highest legislative body of the land and a man used to making fine distinctions between guilty and not guilty, between legitimate and illegitimate. Yet the Judaism which he represented had by his day become a thing of rules and regulations, not devoid by any means of spiritual content, but with that spiritual content heavily overlaid with a kind of religious and moral protocol.

Nicodemus goes to Jesus by night for the obvious

reason that it might be considered rather odd by his peers – he a learned master of the law thought to be consorting with an ignorant Galilean – like an Archbishop sneaking down the road to talk to a young itinerant evangelist of some out of the way sect. It was remarkable of course that he went at all, but presumably he went under the pressure of his own inner ambiguity created by his consciousness of his own status as a qualified teacher of the law and the sterility of his own inner life. He expects, and indeed no doubt hopes for, a learned academic discussion in which he would be at an advantage.

Jesus, while by no means unlearned himself, is not prepared to discuss things at this level and insists, in those famous words, that Nicodemus needs to be 'born again'. Our Lord is drawing his attention to the fact that it is not the status he enjoys nor the experience he acquired, but what he is which matters in the sight of God.

But how can any man help being what he is? He is the product of his own actions, of his own attitudes, of his physical and intellectual inheritance, of his ethnic origins and of his cultural environment. To some extent he can control what he does and what he says. He cannot control what he is. This, our Lord insists, is the crucial matter, and it is for this reason that he has to be 'born again'. Only God can do it for him. He cannot do it for himself.

The decalogue at first sight looks like a catalogue – a catalogue of things to do and not to do, a catalogue of virtues and vices. But the first and the tenth Commandments, if none of the others, make it clear that the moral principles of the universe are exhibited or denied, not in what a man says or does, but in what he is.

When Nicodemus visited Jesus by night and was admitted to His company, he had in his hand a golden string which, thank God, he never entirely let go. He lacked the heroism to become a disciple or indeed to take any very positive steps to save Jesus from false charges. But he did have the courage (and it took courage in the political climate of his day) to identify himself with Jesus by joining Joseph of Arimathaea in claiming the body after the Crucifixion.

He may have been relieved, of course, that this troubler of his conscience was now dead but he probably knew himself well enough to know that he would never forget that midnight hour in which he had visited Jesus and exposed himself to the Word of God. The law would never again be enough for him; only the spirit would do. Never again would he find refuge in his own status or his qualifications. He would never rest until by a mighty act of God he was born again and became a new man.

We do not know what happened to Nicodemus although legends abound. But Clive Sansom ends his poem on Nicodemus with these words:

Only, some evenings, when the night wind blows,
My spirit stirs again, and I remember.

I feel, though I cannot prove, that Nicodemus kept hold of the end of the golden string and found his way in at heaven's gate built in Jerusalem's wall.

12 THE GOLDEN STRING

We have been winding in this golden string for a long time. Are we any nearer heaven's gate, that is to that source of wisdom and grace of which we perceive our need in this very confusing world? The Ten Commandments are not to be regarded as comprehensive statements of the whole duty of man so that if we keep them to the letter we shall be all right. They are starting points at which we become aware of our needs and temptations and follow the hints given to us as we pursue them to their logical conclusion – the end of a golden string. They are Commandments, offering broad guidelines for society as a whole, in our relationships with other societies; relationships, for example, between the developed and the underdeveloped, between Western and Eastern, between black and white, between rich and poor. But before these can become effective for society as a whole they have to be honoured by individuals.

The Commandments are not about how other people should treat us but how we should treat them. It is no good blaming the government for not providing adequate resources for the care of the aged if you do not honour your own parents. Two years ago in this country there was a strike by hospital employees in pursuit of better wages and conditions (which indeed they deserved). This meant that some hospitals and nursing homes had to be closed temporarily and their occupants sent home.

The leader of the union which had called the strike was furious when his mother was sent home and he had to look after her himself. He had a just cause, namely the furtherance of the rights of his members, but he was reluctant to honour the fifth Commandment.

Likewise, it is no good to hold up hands of horror at the details of some sordid murder being rehearsed in court if you habitually nurture anger against your brother. No good lamenting the divorce statistics if you are promiscuous yourself. No good condemning crime if you make a little on the side for yourself. No good berating the newspapers for making misleading statements if you yourself are devious and unreliable in your relationships with other people. No good going on about the rate of inflation if your own firm is making wholly unjustifiable profits.

In the end, therefore, it all comes back to you, the individual 'What shall *I* do to inherit eternal life?', the young man said, or in other words, how am *I* going to find heaven's gate? Or to put it in a more generalised way, which would apply to everyone here on earth, believer or unbeliever – what is my ultimate goal? What destination do I have in my mind? People sometimes say, 'It is better to travel hopefully than to arrive.' But we cannot even travel hopefully without some implicit or explicit objective.

This issue was highlighted for me by a notable film which was showing in London in the summer of 1980. It was called *Meetings with Remarkable Men*, directed by the famous English film director Peter Brook. It was obviously not intended for a mass audience because it was being shown in a cinema holding only sixty people at a time, and it was unimaginably difficult to find out the times of performance or the price of the seats. That was a pity, because it was one of the most beautiful and thought-provoking films that I have ever seen.

It described the life of a man named Gurdjieff, a Russian thinker, who was born in Alexandrapol in 1877 and who died in 1949. He was trained both as a priest and as a physician. He left revolutionary Russia already disabused of the ideals which it embraced and finding Marxism wholly irrelevant to his basic need. His basic need was to experience the ultimate reality and on the basis of that ultimate reality to discover the secret of a universal brotherhood.

The film, which was largely made on location in a mountainous region of Afghanistan, opened with a striking sequence describing a competition which was held every ten years in that locality in which musicians and singers competed with each other in a particular valley which was famous for its resonance. It was the man who made the valley re-echo by the notes he played or sung who won the prize. So in turn they took their stand in the natural auditorium which the valley provided, played their musical instruments and sang their songs. And then after one particular performance came the magic moment when indeed the valley and mountains echoed and re-echoed to the melody which had been played and the competition was over.

The symbolism was at the same time subtle and obvious. It described the 'competition' in which every man may take part in this life as he pursues his own particular resonance with God, with nature and with people. It was describing pictorially the search for truth, the pursuit after reality, or as Blake put it 'heaven's gate'.

The second great concern of Gurdjieff's was 'universal brotherhood' and this was illustrated in another striking sequence. Gurdjieff and another young student were competing for the affections of the same girl and they often came to blows about her. 'There is no room on earth for both of us,' said Gurdjieff to his fellow-student, and they devised a bizarre method of deciding the issue. They went to the local artillery range, hid themselves in the shell holes and waited for the artillery to open up. He who survived would be the winner.

In fact they both survived, although Gurdjieff's rival was badly injured. The sequence ended with a shot of the young man in bed being tended by Gurdjieff himself. There *was* room on earth for both of them. Universal brotherhood was not just a dream.

And so Gurdjieff set off on his life's pursuit, meeting many remarkable men in the process and learning from them valuable lessons for the spiritual life. But he was never satisfied. He felt there was something more and he went on winding in the golden string through many perils and disappointments, many setbacks and betrayals, until he happened upon the guide who was to take him to the source of all truth. This last part of the journey was on horseback with Gurdjieff blindfolded so that he would never be able to betray the whereabouts of the place; they travelled until they came to a chasm across which was a narrow, precarious rope bridge. He crossed it and found himself in a community which claimed acquaintance with the ultimate truth.

And there the film ended, as indeed it had to, but it was so constructed as to leave haunting questions in the mind – was this really the last place, was this really heaven's gate, or did the truth lie even further away, always beckoning the seeker but never divulging its secrets to him? Was this the resonance which Gurdjieff had been so heroically pursuing, or was it just another stage on the way?

There was something heroic about Gurdjieff, as indeed there has always been something heroic about those who have sacrificed everything in pursuit of the ultimate reality. Such men are to be found in every religious tradition and in every philosophical school. Judaism, the bearer of the Ten Commandments to our own day, was to prove itself a heroic religion. Down the centuries most Jewish people, most of the time, were at risk simply by being Jewish, a member of the Chosen race. Of course some of them achieved wealth and worldly power, but for many of them life was a painful unceasing struggle for survival in a series of alien environments.

On a recent visit to Israel I had the opportunity of visiting the famous Diaspora Museum in Tel Aviv. It was a masterpiece of technical wizardry, but the prevailing impression was of a people scattered over the earth, persecuted, hounded from place to place, compelled to live in ghettoes and often deprived of any professional means of making a living. We think of the holocaust in which millions of Jews died in Nazi Germany, but this was only a tiny part of what Jews had suffered for the best part of three thousand years. Who would want to be a chosen people on those terms?

But there is another kind of heroism, less obvious perhaps, but even more demanding. If you go to Jerusalem and visit the ultra-orthodox Jewish quarter called Mea Shearim, you will find a group of people who stand rigorously over against the State of Israel having nothing to do with it and who, day in day out, pursue the study of the Holy Scriptures to the exclusion of almost any other activity. They believe, as Jesus Himself said of them, that they will find in those Scriptures 'eternal life', and they bend every muscle of heart and mind to their task. It is not just a question of learning the Scriptures, or even understanding them, it is a question of living in total detailed obedience to them; so that every action, every word, every thought is consciously made subject to the will of God as they perceive that will of God in the Scriptures. We may think the pursuit perverse but it is heroic in its subjugation of everything on earth to one all-conquering objective.

It was a man from a similar community who ran up to Jesus and kneeling before him said:

> "Good teacher," he asked, "what must I do to inherit eternal life?"
>
> "Why do you call me good," Jesus answered. "No one is good – except God alone. You know the commandments: Do not murder, do not commit adultery, do not steal, do not give false testimony, do not defraud, honour your father and mother."
>
> "Teacher," he declared, "all these I have kept since I was a boy."
>
> Jesus looked at him and loved him. "One thing you lack," he said. "Go, sell everything you have and give to the poor, and you will have treasure in heaven. Then come, follow me."
>
> At this the man's face fell. He went away sad, because he had great wealth.
>
> (Mark 10:17–22)

This was a man of impeccable life who, he supposed, had kept the Ten Commandments. He may have been mistaken of course; he may have been more successful in keeping them in the letter than in the spirit. Nevertheless he represented a kind of heroic piety which was widely admired in the circles in which he moved and which, so he had been taught, was the road to eternal life. But he would not have come to Jesus at all if he had been totally satisfied with the prescription which orthodox Judaism had given him.

Here he was, a good man who had kept the law, but he still seemed a long way from heaven's gate, from eternal life, from the ultimate objective to which many others like himself, and like Gurdjieff, aspired. He clearly perceived in Jesus something that he wanted for himself. What could it have been — a kind of joy and peace and confidence, an ability to understand and relate to other people, an overwhelming sense of the presence of God in Him? He no doubt expected, like a man doing the round of his doctors, just another prescription, another set of rules, a deeper understanding of the Scriptures, a new clue to the meaning of life. The answer he received was not in any of those categories and was wholly astonishing — 'One thing you lack. Go, sell everything you have and give to the poor, and you will have treasure in heaven. Then come, follow me.' (Mark 10:21)

The answer would have been astonishing to the man because he was being asked to do something which, in some ways, seemed a softer option. Our Lord's attitude to the law was much less rigorous than that of most of contemporary Rabbis. He did not insist on rigid adherence to the rules about ritual purity, He sometimes allowed His disciples to break the Sabbath, He did not keep Himself isolated from the common people, from the sick and the mad and the bad, and He taught the law not by the painfully repetitive methods common in the day but by an appeal to everyday and familiar circumstance. Indeed He was known as a glutton and a winebibber, who spent too much of His time at parties. To become, therefore, a member of His group was not, so it seemed, to accept an extreme ascetic way of life such as that accepted by the Essenes, for example, or the Qumran sect.

The man had been a follower of Moses, seeking to apply in the greatest detail the mandates which came down from Sinai. Now he is being asked to follow Jesus, as if this were somehow an alternative and higher way of life, the royal road to heaven's gate. The whole mighty edifice of law and regulation by which the loyal Jew lived was now subsumed under one command – follow Jesus of Nazareth. Jesus was no mighty warrior of the faith, no great statesman refined in the fires of experience and adversity; He had wrought no great deliverance for Israel, had not led them on any 'long march', and as far as could be known had not received any command from God on some awesome mountain somewhere. His face did not shine with the glory of God. In short, Jesus was no Moses, but a young man who had been in a small way of business in an unattractive northern town, whose ministry even now extended for no more than two or three years and had gathered to Himself in that time a small, and to tell the truth, a rather disreputable group of disciples. He was not offering a kind of Promised Land at the end of a long march, He was notably reticent about His attitude to their Roman overlords, and He had not summoned His followers to blood and fire and heroic deeds. So to be told that the prescription for eternal life was to join Himself on to this rather odd little group of people was astonishing to the young man.

Astonishing, yes, but the trouble was that it was true. In that casual encounter on the other side of Jordan a man had been offered the end of a golden string and he had failed to pick it up. He might have become an Apostle, he could have evangelised Rome or India, established churches in Asia Minor; he might have won great battles of faith in Greece, but more important than all these, he would have found eternal life. The long pursuit in which he had sacrificially engaged came to a grinding halt. He goes sorrowfully away and we hear no more of him.

Jesus embodies in His own person the proper objective of every human soul. He does not abolish the Ten Commandments. They remain for ever, as He said, the Word of God, but He enriches them and articulates them in a way peculiar to Himself, far beyond the range reached anywhere else in Judaism. With Him as interpreter they become a rich source for the guiding of corporate and personal life.

But of course He is more than a teacher of the law, pointing His hearers to eternal life and showing them the way. He *is* the way. Life is not just some long heroic pilgrimage of a Gurdjieff sort, culminating in some attainment down the long years of a man's life – distant, remote, indescribable, the other side of a chasm with only a narrow rope bridge across.

To come to Christ is to enjoy in that very coming 'eternal life'. 'He that has seen me,' Jesus said to one of His disciples, 'has seen the Father.' We encounter God in Jesus Christ. He is the other end of the golden string. When we reach Him we are at heaven's gate, built in Jerusalem's wall.

Those of you who are seriously engaged on the quest for truth, your souls restless until you find it, could do worse than listen to the words of Jesus Himself –

Come to me all you who are weary and burdened and I will give you rest. Take my yoke upon you and learn from me for I am gentle and humble in

133

heart and you will find rest for your souls, for my yoke is easy and my burden is light.

(Matt. 11:28–30)

13 CONCLUSION

It is with some relief that the writer of a book, having dotted the last 'i' and crossed the last 't' and having, as he believes, remedied every omission and corrected every mistake, puts the typescript into an envelope and sends it off to the publisher. But with that sense of relief goes also an acute apprehension, for now his follies and his errors and his lack of judgement are to be exposed to the world. I am aware, for example, that I have not entered into any historical discussion of the events at Sinai from which the Ten Commandments are said to proceed. That is partly because the historical issues were fully discussed in my previous book, *The Trumpet in the Morning,* and partly because no discussion, however exhaustive, can recover the past with any certainty. All we can say with confidence is, these Commandments are part of an ancient historical tradition which has been proved to be in its main outlines reliable, and which remains part of the living faith of Judaism. Moreover, I am acquainted with only a tiny part of the vast literature which attends to or is derived from the study of the Ten Commandments, both within the Jewish tradition and outside it. This would be a life's work in itself and would have produced a book of immense size and complexity.

Furthermore, and this is especially true of any book which begins as a series of addresses, my own prejudices will inevitably show through. But there is nothing I can do about my prejudices except exhibit them and hope that someone who has a different set of prejudices will in due course attempt the same task. So it is with some trepidation that I put this script into the envelope and write the name of the publishers on the front.

However, I am emboldened by the fact that throughout the academic studies which lie behind the book and the detailed preparation that produced the broadcast script my two basic convictions about the subject in hand have not only survived — they have deepened and enlarged. And they are these. First, that there is an important connection between law and freedom which we ignore at our peril. The vagaries of the human mind are such that we need some standards outside ourselves by which to judge our personal or collective decisions. Whatever doubts we may have about the historical events surrounding the giving of the law we can have no doubts about their effects on the people of Israel. The law, to them, was not a series of deductions from their own experience, nor was it an arbitrary system imposed upon them by their rulers. The law was a gift of God, unchangeable, unchanging, which stood over against them in all the perplexities and misunderstandings of a constantly changing historical scene. The Hebrew people lived out their lives, whether in Palestine or Babylon or Egypt or Rome, under the shadow of Sinai, seeing the flames and hearing the voice.

The second conviction is that this law in all its grandeur and antiquity has been once in the history of mankind perfectly expressed in the life and teaching of Jesus of Nazareth. This is a claim which my Jewish friends would, of course, dispute. If I dissent from them I do so with a vivid sense of my own debt to the ancient people of God who have preserved the law, lived by it and died for it, over the course of the centuries, down to our own day. But I have to dissent from them nevertheless on the basis of the New Testament (largely written, we have to note, by Jews) which asserts, or at least implies, that Jesus was regarded by His contemporaries as a teacher of the law, who took as His own datum point the giving of the law to Moses at Sinai. He differed, however, from the other teachers of the law in His own day in insisting that law was a gift of a loving father rather than a stern judge, to be received and obeyed in a spirit of joy and freedom.

So my last word must be that I do not regard the Ten Commandments as a burden on our consciences or a restriction of our freedom, but as the God-given way by which under the guidance of the Spirit we do God's will, experience His power and see His glory. I look for the dawn which rose that day over Sinai and will rise again over a world healed of its infirmities and radiant with hope.